Traynham

61-10514

5-4-62

Ancient Peoples and Places

CZECHOSLOVAKIA

General Editor

DR GLYN DANIEL

Ancient Peoples and Places

CZECHOSLOVAKIA

BEFORE THE SLAVS

Evžen and Jiří Neustupný

88 PHOTOGRAPHS
52 LINE DRAWINGS
2 MAPS AND 3 CHARTS

FREDERICK A. PRAEGER
New York

THIS IS VOLUME TWENTY-TWO IN THE SERIES

Ancient Peoples and Places

GENERAL EDITOR: DR GLYN DANIEL

BOOKS THAT MATTER

*Published in the United States of America
in 1961 by Frederick A. Praeger, Inc.
Publisher, 64 University Place
New York 3, N.Y.
All rights reserved
Library of Congress Catalog Card Number: 61–10514
© Thames and Hudson London
Printed in Great Britain by Jarrold and Sons Ltd. Norwich*

CONTENTS

ILLUSTRATIONS

7

9

10

CHAPTER I

The Natural Background

THE elongated shape of Czechoslovakia makes it extend from the middle of Central Europe far towards the east, so con- necting two regions that are of great importance in the develop- ment of prehistoric Europe: Central Europe and the Carpathian basin. In prehistoric times Czechoslovakia often acted as an intermediary between Central and North Europe on the one hand and the advanced Balkan regions on the other hand, and new cultural innovations passed through it to the northern regions.

During the last thousand years covered by written records Czechoslovakia has become divided into three parts: Bohemia, Moravia, and Slovakia, the first and second inhabited by the Czechs, the third by the closely related Slovaks.

The westernmost part, Bohemia, has formed a historical unit ever since the end of the tenth century. It is enclosed by distinct geographical boundaries. In the south-west it is hemmed in by the impenetrable ridges of the Šumava Mountains (maximum elevation 1457 metres) and the Bohe- mian Forest (Böhmerwald), in the north-west by the Ore Mountains (Erzgebirge) (maximum elevation 1244 metres) rich in tin deposits, while in the north-east the Giant Mountains (maximum elevation 1603 metres) and the Orlice Mountains form the frontiers with Poland. The south-east bordering upon Moravia is occupied by the extensive Bohemio-Moravian Highlands (Českomoravská vysočina) which though not high (maximum elevation 837 metres) are characterized by a rather harsh climate.

From the standpoint of prehistoric development Bohemia was often divided into two parts. The northern, consisting of the region drained by the rivers Labe (Elbe), the Lower Vltava,

Fig 1 Sketch-map of Czechoslovakia

the Ohře, and the Bělá, has been densely populated since
Neolithic times. It is gently undulating (with the exception of
the volcanic České středohoří Mountains), and its soil consists
mainly of loess-loams. The southern highlands, on the other
hand, were not inhabited until the Middle Bronze Age and
even then only thinly. They are hilly and even today covered

with forests growing on poorer soils which are ill-suited to agriculture. In comparison with the northern part of the country, the climate there is much rougher. In the Bohemio-Moravian Highlands and the other mountainous regions continuous settlement did not take place until the Early Middle Ages.

There were not many routes by which prehistoric settlers

could enter the country. One way leading from Regensburg in the direction of Plzeň has been known since the Neolithic period, another, also from the west, along the valley of the river Ohře was frequented in the Mesolithic and Eneolithic periods and the Bronze Age. A very important route followed the river Labe (Elbe) to East Germany. Of minor importance were the ways from Lusatia via Liberec to North-East Bohemia. The route from Silesia over Kladsko has ever and again been used. However, most important of all were the passages across the Bohemio-Moravian Highlands which connected Bohemia and Moravia and probably took the same route as today's railway line. This was the way by which the first Neolithic agriculturalists entered Bohemia, and since that time its importance has not diminished.

MORAVIA

The last-mentioned way brings us to Moravia which, within today's frontiers, has formed a historical unit for about as long as Bohemia. In the north it is bordered by the Jeseníky Mountains (maximum elevation 1490 metres) the northern slopes of which represent the Czechoslovak part of Silesia, in the east by the westernmost bend of the Carpathian range (maximum elevation 1325 metres) and in the west by the above-mentioned Bohemio-Moravian Highlands. In the south Moravia is open to Austria and the adjacent part of Slovakia. Besides westward connexions with Bohemia the so-called Moravian Gateway—a wide thoroughfare between the east spurs of the Jeseníky Mountains and the western bend of the Carpathians—was of the greatest importance for the colonization of southern Poland and sometimes even of the regions farther to the east. It was one of the principal arteries of prehistoric Europe. Geographically Moravia is divided into three regions which, covered with fertile loess, have been inhabited continuously since the Neolithic Age. One of them is situated in the north on the banks of the Upper Morava river, another, the so-called southern Moravia, spreads from the river Dyje (Thaya) northwards in the direction of Brno, and the third covers the valley of the lower course of the river Morava (Eastern Moravia). The two latter have many connexions with the Carpathian basin.

The invasion of the Magyars at the beginning of the tenth century separated Slovakia from the western part of Czecho-slovakia of today, and it has had a different historic develop-ment ever since. In prehistory also it often belonged to different cultural spheres from Bohemia and Moravia. It forms a more or less pronounced geographical unit in the north of the Carpathian basin, the greater part of the country being taken up by the mountain ranges of the Carpathians (maximum elevation 2663 metres) and in prehistory only sporadically inhabited. Two regions of outstanding fertility are recognizable on the map: the lowland of South-West Slovakia (north of the Danube) and the lowland of East Slovakia. Both these regions opening in the south to the Carpathian basin have been un-interruptedly inhabited since the earliest Neolithic Age. The connexions of Slovakia with the west were of momentous importance: nearly all the cultural innovations coming from the Balkans to Central Europe had to pass the country between the north-eastern slopes of the Alps and the south-western end of the Carpathian bow—just that stretch of land between Bratislava and Vienna. The passages across the Carpathians leading from Slovakia to the south of Poland have also been known since Neolithic times at least.

The prehistoric inhabitants of Czechoslovakia confined them-selves to the regions favoured by climate and from the Neolithic Age, to those with fertile soils as well. Settlements were but seldom situated higher than four hundred metres above sea-level and avoided heavy loams, stony grounds, slightly weathered sands, or badly drained soils. Stretches of loess-loams have been continuously populated since the Neolithic Age but in the mountainous districts permanent settlements did not appear until the Middle Ages.

PLEISTOCENE The development of the climate at the time when prehistoric man inhabited Czechoslovakia of today is relatively well known. During the Pleistocene this territory, as well as the rest of Central Europe, was under the influence of eleven successive glaciations which the geologists have grouped into four glacial phases (Günz, Mindel, Riss, Würm). In the Early Pleistocene the conditions were favourable to human life as the climate was very mild. It was not until the Late Pleistocene that the influence of periglacial phenomena was felt which, unfortunately, destroyed the layers formed during the preceding periods, and with them probably also many of the oldest traces of mankind. The Scandinavian glaciers reached the northern boundaries of Czechoslovakia only twice: in the middle of the third glacial phase (Riss) and perhaps also at the end of the Mindel phase. Local glaciers appeared on the Ore Mountains, the Giant Mountains, and the Carpathians. During the last, the Würm phase, three glaciations occurred, the first of which was separated from the second by a very warm interval, while a rather cold climate prevailed between the second and the third glaciation. Yet it was just at that time that very characteristic and matured cultures of mammoth-hunters developed in the territory of Czechoslovakia.

HOLOCENE After the last Ice Age the climate grew warmer, the waste stretches of the periglacial tundras disappeared, and forests began to cover the country. The spread of forests passed through several stages in the course of which many plants and animals that require a warm climate penetrated into the north. In Pre-Boreal times, about 8000 B.C., birch and pine forests grew here; in the following Boreal phase hazel and mixed oak forests joined them. The Atlantic period was moist and warm, and the mixed oak forests prevailed. This was the milieu in which Mesolithic man lived. In the later part of the

Atlantic period—about 4000 B.C.—the territory of Czecho slovakia was already inhabited by the earliest Neolithic farmers. At the beginning of the third millennium, in the Eneolithic period a still warm but dry Sub-Boreal climate set in, beech trees appeared more often in the forests, and fir trees spread on the higher levels, though the mixed oak forests continued to hold their ground side by side with them. These climatic con ditions lasted until Hallstatt times to be again succeeded by a moist (Sub-Atlantic) climate which, finally, in historic times, gave way to conditions corresponding to those of today.

In prehistory the forest formed the dominant feature of man's visible surroundings. Tree-clearing did not begin until the Neolithic Age, spread somewhat in Hallstatt times but was not able to change the character of the country until the later Middle Ages.

CLIMATE AND MAN

The climate influenced the activities of prehistoric man in two ways; firstly, by putting obstacles in his way which were sometimes insurmountable (for example, glaciers); secondly, by regulating the character of the flora and fauna that made up his environment. In the territory of Czechoslovakia the warm Atlantic climate was certainly a precondition for the settlement of farmers, but the causes of the change to a Neolithic economy lay elsewhere. The later changes of the weather conditions were each of decreasing importance as by then prehistoric man was able to adapt himself to them. Thus the importance of the natural environment diminished gradually as the armament of knowledge of prehistoric man increased.

CHAPTER II

The Earliest Inhabitants of Czechoslovakia

THE LOWER PALAEOLITHIC PERIOD
FROM ABOUT 600,000 TO 150,000 B.C.

U P to the present there has been no evidence to suggest that the territory of Czechoslovakia belongs to that part of the world where, at the beginning of the Quarternary, the process of the origin of man took place.

THE FIRST
TOOLS

The oldest tool worked by man found in Czechoslovakia is a flake discovered in a fluvial terrace of the first or second glacial phase at Seňa I in East Slovakia. Another flake produced in the same technique, the so-called Clactonian, and found at Letky near Prague is probably somewhat later.

EFFECTS OF
GLACIATION

The very mild climate of Central Europe preceding the third glacial phase (Riss) was very favourable to human life. It allowed also a diversity of fauna which was never to be seen again because during the Riss phase the climate deteriorated and many species became extinct. The colossal earth-movements of the third glacial phase buried a great deal of the top-soil of the older Pleistocene, thus depriving us of many traces of prehistoric man in the territory of Czechoslovakia.

STONE
INDUSTRY

From this phase (Riss) come some further finds, geologically precisely datable but unfortunately very difficult to classify from the archaeological point of view. They are made of local, poor-quality raw materials (quartz, quartzite) and are typologically not sufficiently characteristic for us to be able to assign them to any of the known classic Early Palaeolithic phases of the adjoining parts of West or East Europe. And as chance would have it, the finds which *can* be classified do not come from geologically datable strata, as for instance, the hand-axe from

Křešice in North Bohemia, and some other, mainly Moravian, finds.

In Czechoslovakia as well as in the other parts of the world remains of Early Palaeolithic man are scarce and their variety is limited. There are very few standard types of stone implements (choppers, hand-axes, flakes) but they are very significant, as their repeated production demonstrates that man of that time already had standardized conceptions and consequently also abstract notions. Abstract thinking being impossible without a language we must presume that its beginnings existed already at that time. As we do not know of any settlement or other remains, however, except some dispersed stone implements, we are not able to say much about these earliest inhabitants of Czechoslovakia. Judging from finds from other parts of the world we may presume that they knew fire, hunted all the animals that could be attacked with the primitive weapons at their disposal, and certainly also gathered vegetable food. Some organization into primitive societies of at least a temporary character must also be taken for granted as, after the spread of early man into 'secondary habitats' with scarce food resources, this was the only way in which he could survive. The earliest man did not yet know either religion or art, and no traces of his spiritual culture have been left.

ABSTRACT
THOUGHT

ECONOMY AND
SOCIETY

CHAPTER III

The Beginnings of Modern Man

THE MIDDLE PALAEOLITHIC AND THE
BEGINNING OF THE UPPER PALAEOLITHIC PERIOD
FROM ABOUT 150,000 TO 40,000 B.C.

NEANDERTHAL
MAN

THE last interglacial (Riss-Würm) and the first interstadial epoch of the Würm phase were very warm but the climate of its first and second stadial was rigorous, although it did not drive prehistoric man away from Czechoslovakia for ever. Neither in human evolution nor in climate was this long period uniform. In the course of the interglacial and the first Würm stadial Neanderthal Man, a development of *Pithecanthropus*, appeared. His skeletal remains have been found at several places in Czechoslovakia, most important being a travertine endocast of a skull from Gánovce in Slovakia (last interglacial) and a child's jaw from the Šipka cave in Moravia (beginning of the last glacial). But already in the second stadial of the Würm phase we meet with a characteristic *Homo sapiens* in the finds from Koněprusy near Prague.

PROGRESS OF
PRODUCTION

In spite of the climatic and anthropologic diversity, from the standpoint of basic cultural traits this era appears uniform: it marks the beginning of the specialization of stone implements on the basis of the newly developing blade technique, the beginning of the specialized hunting of gregarious animals, obviously also the beginnings of a firm organization of society and, above all, it shows the first traces of religion and art.

MOUSTERIAN
CULTURE

In this transitional Mousterio-Aurignacian period the Mousterian culture is the older one. We are as yet unable to trace its origin because of the scarcity of finds from the preceding period. Settlements in the open air as well as in caves have been

20

discovered. They are datable geologically in the last interglacial and the first stadial of the Würm phase. The stone implements have already attained a certain perfection of shape and specialization. We can distinguish various types of points, side-scrapers and, perhaps, even end-scrapers. Different knives of unretouched flakes were certainly of equal importance. These implements are either made by the complicated Levalloisian technique which had already appeared outside Czechoslovak territory in the Lower Palaeolithic period or, more often, by the Mousterian technique (faceted striking planes on disc-cores) derived from the former. Both these techniques signified great progress in the production of stone implements and prepared the way for the blade technique which, however, is still very seldom met with in the Mousterian period. For Czechoslovak sites the choice of material for stone implements was usually limited to local stones with poor cleavage (quartz, quartzite, and so on), though we sometimes meet also with chert and flint. The poor typological quality of this industry is the result of these unsuitable raw materials. It seems probable that some little hand-axes which we know only from isolated finds belong to the Mousterian culture. From them the flat, leaf-shaped points (*pointes foliacées*), so characteristic of the closely following period may have developed.

Fig. 2

Fig. 2 Mousterian tools: (a) side-scraper, (b) point. Švédův stůl cave, Moravian Karst, near Brno. 2:3

21

AURIGNACIAN
CULTURE

The end of the Mousterian period is much better understood than its beginning. The Aurignacian culture, which began in Czechoslovak territory in the first interstadial of the Würm phase, carries on many traditions of the preceding Mousterian culture. Often it assumes the character of a typical blade-culture (in contrast to the preceding flake-cultures) but it must be pointed out not only that blades had already been met with before (for example, Mousterian at Lobkovice) but also that they do not in fact predominate among the earliest Aurignacian finds (as at Barca).

SPECIALIZED
TOOLS
Fig. 3

The new blade technique consisted in detaching long thin blades of which various specialized implements were made. This new method was so efficient that it was never surpassed and it continued to be used until the end of the Stone Age. Besides points and side-scrapers we meet also carinated and end-scrapers, and in isolated cases even burins and borers. The most perfect implements are the so-called Szeletian flat points in the shape of leaves of various trees (laurel, willow, etc.) finished with surface retouching. Generally they are considered as characteristic of the so-called Szeletian culture. For the first time bone objects make their appearance—points of the Mladeč type (in the preceding Mousterian period bones were only used in the manufacture of stone tools).

| a | b | c | d | e |

Fig. 3   Aurignaco-Szeletian stone industry: (a) plane-shaped scraper, (b) end-scraper, (c) notched blade, (d) point, (e) Szeletian point. Žlutava (a) and Kvasice (b, c, and d), Moravia; Dzeravá skala, Slovakia (e). 2:3

In some recent archaeological works two contemporary cultures are said to have flourished in Central Europe at this time: the Aurignacian coming from the east, and the Szeletian, which developed from the local Mousterian culture. But the greater part of the inventory of the two cultures is identical and even the types considered as diagnostic—leaf-shaped points and carinated scrapers for the Szeletian and Aurignacian cultures respectively—appear often together at the same site. As it is most unlikely that two populations with different cultures should have lived some ten thousand years unamalgamated on the same territory, the present writers consider them as a cultural whole with two, presumably seasonal, variants.

The Aurignacians lived in cave as well as in open-air settlements. At Barca near Košice (East Slovakia) a whole settlement complex (subterranean pit-dwellings with traces of posts supporting roofs) has even been brought to light. Dated to the first Würm interstadial it represents the oldest of all known architectural remains. At Moravany in West Slovakia a settlement has been discovered with floors of crosswise laid beams—again an example of a developed architecture.

Evidence of hunting exists at many places. Various animals, among them the mammoth, the reindeer, and the bear were hunted. Near the settlement of Barca was an accumulation of bones bearing witness to the hunting of large herd animals. The collection of vegetable food must certainly also have been important, but so far no evidence has been forthcoming.

From the Aurignacian culture come also the first traces of art. Fragments of bone with incisions and an engraving of (perhaps) a fish on the rib of a mammoth have been found at Holedeč in Bohemia. This period has also yielded a bone whistle and a necklace made of dentalia (little tube-like shells) as well as a perforated shell of a marine *Molluscum*. The discovery of red and yellow colours with which prehistoric man perhaps adorned his body has been reported from some

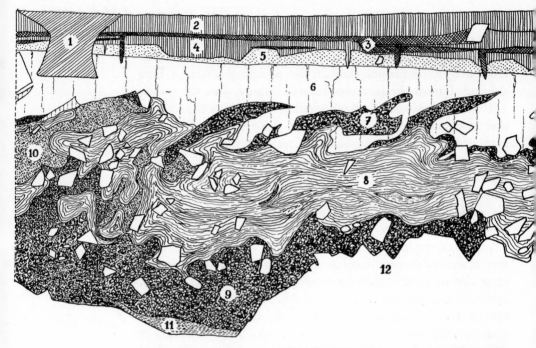

Fig. 4 Dzeravá skala cave, S.W. Slovakia, section: 1–4, layers with Neolithic finds; 5, travertine layer, Atlantic period; 6, loess, Würm 3, with Late Gravettian in upper part of layer; 7, dark-grey clay touched by frost, beginning of the tundra phase, Würm 3, with Gravettian at base of layer; 8, greenish- to brownish-grey clay, Würm 2, Aurignaco-Szeletian; 9, rocky clay, approx. Würm 1; 10, loamy clay; 11, clay with coarse stones; 12, base-rock. c. 1:40

settlements. All these objects, many of them reliably dated in the geological sequence, are among the most ancient proofs of artistic activity.

RELIGION   In close connexion with art was religion. The above-mentioned whistle and colours were most probably used in the course of religious rites. The necklaces of dentalia as well as the image of the fish might also have had a magic significance. The burials undoubtedly point to a belief in an after-life. The well-known grave containing the bodies of twenty persons in an abandoned hut at Předmostí near Přerov, for instance, was lined with shoulder-blades and jaws of mammoths and covered with a forty-centimetre thick layer of stones. From a cave at Mladeč in Moravia traces of cannibalism have been reported.

While the members of the preceding Mousterian culture had been Neanderthal men, the bodies from the Aurignacian graves (Předmostí, Koněprusy) are already *Homo sapiens*.

The collective hunting of big animals which dates from the Mousterian period must without any doubt have considerably raised the standard of living. It required not only the improve-ment of hunting technique and the development of imple-ments in order to take rapid advantage of the big kill, but also a far more complex communal organization. We may suppose that it was in this period that the natural division of labour, necessary in such a difficult attempt, has its origin. On the basis of this natural division of labour a marked separa-tion of the generations as well as of the sexes must have taken place for the first time. In this way a society could originate which, later on, would lead to the formation of the tribal organization with forms strictly based on kinship.

SUMMARY

In religious ideas a similar development can be traced. The simple belief in an after-life led to ritual burials and the most ancient traces of art point to other aspects of religion, especially magic. All this evidence may seem slight if we compare it with the richness of the following Gravettian period. Yet it was the Mousterio-Aurignacian epoch which laid the firm founda-tion for the further development of mankind: it brought a new physical form of man, a new way of hunting, a new stone in-dustry, and a higher specialization of implements, the first bone implements, the first architecture, the elements of tribal organiza-tion and, last but not least, the first elements of religion and art based on achievements in the economic and social fields.

CHAPTER IV

The Hunters of the Upper Palaeolithic Period

FROM ABOUT 40,000 TO 10,000 B.C.

THE long history of the Aurignacian culture, dealt with in the preceding chapter, shows an outstanding advance. At its end, still in the second stadial of the Würm phase, we discover in the settlements the so-called 'Gravettian points' and other elements which illustrate the trend towards the Late Palaeolithic Gravettian culture. It may be taken as practically certain, therefore, that this culture originated in Central Europe, although it occurs also in East Europe and is well known in West Europe under the denomination 'Late Perigordian'.

HUNTING OF
HERD ANIMALS
The stone industry shows only an insignificant part of the progress attained by the people of the Central European Gravettian culture in the last glacial phase. The specialized hunting of herd animals, especially mammoths but also horses, reindeer, and others, was now firmly established in their economy. This is proved by the large accumulations of bones in the Moravian settlements: the bones of more than a thousand mammoths have been found at Předmostí and the quantities discovered at Dolní Věstonice and Pavlov are not less impressive. The flesh was eaten, the bones used as raw material for the manufacture of implements and the building of dwellings, or

VEGETABLE
FOOD
even served as fuel. The gathering of vegetable food supplemented the one-sided meat diet. Tubers and roots were dug out with hoes and shovels made from bone and, as attested by an engraving on a bone from Dolní Věstonice, some graminaceous plants were already used as food. Like the later Neolithic cultures, the Gravettian occurs mostly on loess soils. This, however, is no reason to suppose the existence of a

Palaeolithic agriculture—it is more probable that the principal game, the mammoth, living mainly in the loess steppes attracted the population there. In the Late Gravettian period we can observe that the change to other beasts of chase caused the dependence of the early men on the loess soils to disappear.

Stone implements could hardly have been effective for the hunt of mammoths, but they were probably used for the killing of lesser animals and the dismembering of the carcass. The javelin was in use at that time, but whether the Gravettian points served as arrow-heads has not yet been established. However, we must suppose that at the end of this period the bow was already known.

HUNTING
WEAPONS

Most of the stone implements are made of morainic flint or chert but radiolarian chert, obsidian, and other local raw materials were also used. Technically the manufacture of long blades for numerous special tools like points, knives, end-scrapers, burins, borers, and combined implements had become predominant. Even the presence of the so-called microliths has been ascertained. As in the following Mesolithic Age, they were obviously used for the production of compound tools through insertion of several of these miniature blades in wood or bone hafts. This many-sided specialization of the tools was evidently

STONE
IMPLEMENTS
Fig. 5

a   b   c

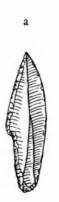

Fig. 5 Gravettian stone industry: (a) *notched point* (à cran) (*Dolní Věstonice, S. Moravia*), (b) *point of Gravettian type* (*Petřkovice, N. Moravia*), (c) *combined scraper-graver* (*Lubná, Central Bohemia*). c. 2:3

27

necessary for the rapid carving up of the kill, and for the manufacture of other implements and objects of bone or wood.

It is supposed that mainly stone burins were used for the
production of the now abundant bone objects, which prove the
perfection of the techniques of splitting, burnishing, and
cutting. The development of shapes, however, was still poor.

An important invention, the many possibilities of which
were left unutilized until the Neolithic Age, was the firing of
clay. At that time it was employed only for the manufacture of
human and animal figurines (the fingerprints in clay of Palaeolithic man, fired presumably by chance in the pottery oven,
have also remained preserved). So far, finds of these oldest
ceramic objects of the world are known only from South
Moravia (at Pavlov and Dolní Věstonice).

Another discovery, one that had to wait longer still for its
exploitation on a large scale, was that coal could be used to
maintain a fire. At Petřkovice, North Moravia, coal has been
found directly in a fire-place to which prehistoric man must have
brought it intentionally from a near-by outcrop.

Most of the implements mentioned so far come from settlements in which the individual dwellings can often be recognized. Partly sunk into the soil, they consisted above ground
of a tent-like construction weighted down with animal bones.
Inside there might be several fire-places, of which probably one
only was used at a time, and a great quantity of rubbish:
bones, stone and bone implements, cult-objects, etc. Sometimes this refuse accumulated at a place outside the dwelling,
probably where the activities of daily life were concentrated
in fine weather. Besides open-air settlements, which later
became covered with loess, caves also were inhabited. But at
that time man was no longer satisfied with their natural shape
and adapted it by means of wood and stone partitions. These
primitive walls in some caves of the Bohemian Karst represent
the most ancient stone constructions in Central Europe.

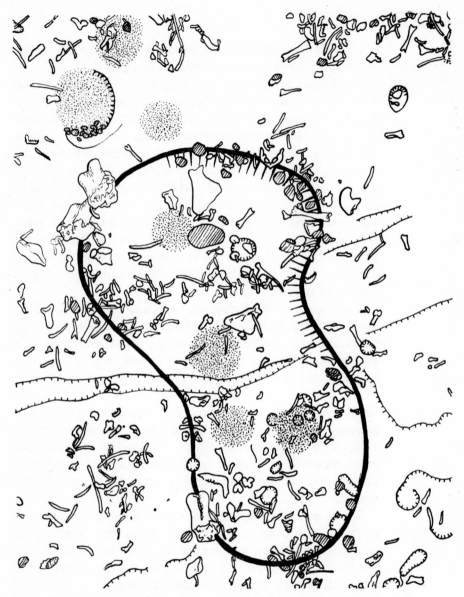

Fig. 6 Pavlov, S. Moravia. Gravettian site. In the hollowed pit, four hearths; on the rims, stones; animal bones concentrated mainly in the pit and its vicinity. c. 1 : 75

By analogy with the development in West Europe, the culture succeeding the classic Gravettian is often called Magdalenian. But in the stone industry as well as in many other aspects we observe a close continuity from the preceding period, and it is therefore more appropriate to call it Late Gravettian. The classic Gravettian appears always covered with loess while the Late Gravettian occupies the end of the glacial phase, a period when the formation of loess had already stopped. We have relatively few remains from this period—which is perhaps a consequence of the comparatively more mobile way of life of these ancient huntsmen, whose principal objects of pursuit were now migrating herds of reindeer, horses, and bison. The hunt has remained as specialized as it was during the classic Gravettian, only as a result of the alteration in the climatic conditions the game had changed.

IMPLEMENTS

The tools, mainly of flint, are functionally differentiated to a considerable degree. Besides various types of knives we again find many kinds of burin, scrapers, points with blunted backs (termed Gravettian), borers, saws, chisels, planes, and other implements. The number of microliths increases and some of these stone tools have remained preserved with their bone hafts. The Late Gravettian brings the development of the bone industry in which points, needles, and especially harpoonheads with rows of barbs figure prominently. The harpoonheads mounted on javelins were certainly as effective weapons as the bow, knowledge of which is generally assumed for this period.

CAMPS

The population of the Late Gravettian camped either in the open air or in caves; the settlements in the latter are very important as it was only there that bone objects and with them works of art could survive—in the open air bones would have perished through the alkaline nature of the soil.

SOCIETY

The process of social change which had probably already begun in the MousterioAurignacian period continued now at a much accelerated pace. The firmly adopted division of labour, prerequisite in a specialized hunting group, must have led to the differentiation of the communities on the basis of sex and age. But the elements of clan organization cannot be supposed to have been fully developed as yet. Be it as it may, this was the decisive period in which the process of the formation of the early human society reached its first peak.

The fundamental social changes that took place at this time left traces in the mentality of prehistoric man. We summarize them under the term 'religion' although here it does not cover the same notion as in later religions but incorporates elements of magic and even of science. But even the realization that there are forces of nature encircling man appears as a great intellectual step forward, since there is no evidence that in former periods people had conceived the universe in any way. The realization of these forces, with which there was often no other way of dealing than the religious one, was certainly stimulated by the better knowledge of nature that man, now an experienced hunter and gatherer had acquired. Those problems that fell within the compass of his knowledge of nature he solved in a rational way and in the other cases religion was an explanation of the inexplicable, something which calmed his apprehension of the impotence of both the individual and the whole community. Thus the progress of human knowledge often assumed a religious form even though its content was quite rational. The hunt was preceded by various rites after which followed action based on experience with animals and knowledge of their reactions.

RELIGION

The most ancient art was inseparable from religion, and included both rational and magical elements. In the territory of Czechoslovakia evidence of Palaeolithic art has remained preserved in many precious objects and every year new finds are added. It is not to be expected that pictures on the walls of caves should be discovered, but the great number of little

MAGIC

objects, mostly made of bone or fired clay and sometimes also of soft stone, richly make up for this. The techniques of their manufacture are of the simplest: carving, engraving, modelling; but the subjects, taken from the everyday life of Paleolithic hunters are all the more varied.

ANIMAL
FIGURINES
Plates 7, 16

Plate 6

Plate 5

During the classic Gravettian nearly all the game, in motion or at rest, is represented in masterly sketches or with full elaboration of all the details either in engravings on flat bones or in fully modelled objects.

The figurine of a bear from Dolní Věstonice shows clearly-recognizable wounds—traces of the magic rite which was to grant that in the following hunt the real bear should get injured in the same way. The stone point of a spear with the engraved design of a lamprey found at Keblice in North-West Bohemia likewise had a magic significance. It is the only known representation of this aquatic parasite in European Palaeolithic art. It was certainly meant to facilitate the tracking of the quarry. The Late Gravettian picture of bison fighting engraved on a bone found in the Pekárna cave in the Moravian Karst near Brno compares advantageously with the best works of art of the West European Magdalenian period. It shows two fighting bulls ramming their heads against each other, their bodies strained at the shock of the impact, and a third bison waiting at a little distance. The bison are covered with magic arrows to facilitate their killing in the next hunt.

VENUSES

Plates 10, 11

The so-called Venuses form a significant, though not very numerous, group in the Gravettian plastic works of art. They are figurines of naked women with accentuated sexual features, sometimes of a considerable perfection of shape. Among them, a figurine modelled in an ash-grey substance, known as the 'Venus of Věstonice', enjoys world repute. From the same site comes also the modelled head of a woman which is remarkable as the face and the head are expressed in detail whereas in the other Venuses this part of the body, which obviously seemed unimportant to prehistoric man, appear strongly schematized. Some of the stylized Venuses probably represent women in travail while other Venuses from Dolní Věstonice are mere sticks with hypertrophic indications of the breasts. The precise function of the Palaeolithic Venuses is not known. They were certainly associated with some cult and probably served in magic rites for increasing fertility.

Plates 4, 8

Plate 13

The various ornaments as well as the painting of bodies with mineral pigments probably had a religious function. Parts of necklaces (teeth, shells, carved pendants) are found in settlements and in graves of which larger numbers are known from this period. Thus about six hundred shells and a male figurine carved in ivory have been found in a grave at Brno. Rare objects like bits of amber, a meteorite, fossil shells etc. probably once served as amulets.

ORNAMENTS
Plates 12 and 14

Plate 9

It is difficult to describe in this short space the whole wealth of the material and spiritual life of the Late Palaeolithic hunters in Czechoslovakia, and to mention all the discoveries with which they enriched mankind. Without any doubt most important of all is their intensive concentration on a certain way of subsistence, taking full advantage of collective collaboration and natural division of labour. It was only on this basis that the first clearly definable forms of society could develop, and the first conception of the universe originate, so perfectly reflected in contemporary works of art.

PROGRESS OF
CULTURE

CHAPTER V

Before the New Age

THE FISHERMEN AND THE HUNTERS OF THE MESOLITHIC
PERIOD FROM THE TENTH TO THE FIFTH MILLENNIUM B.C.

CLIMATIC
CHANGES

A FTER the last retreat of the continental ice-barrier followed a considerably warmer climate accompanied by the return of the warmth-loving fauna and flora from the south. The cold-climate species migrated towards the north and thus the great herd animals, principally reindeer, abandoned the territory of Czechoslovakia. In their stead appeared a rich forest fauna of a great diversity, many sorts of fish populated the rivers and the new natural milieu yielded an abundance and variety of vege-table foods. Although similar natural conditions had already appeared many times before, at the beginning of each inter-glacial, it was only Mesolithic man who was sufficiently equipped by the preceding development of culture to be able to take full advantage of them for the further progress of mankind.

MICROLITHS
AND
COMPOUND
TOOLS

The stone implements of the Late Palaeolithic were suffici-ently differentiated, and it was no difficult task to alter and make them answer any new purpose. The Gravettian trend towards a reduction of the size of stone tools and the use of combined implements culminated in the Mesolithic Age. That is why we speak of microlithic industries in which the single, perfectly worked, little blades were not used independ-ently but were inserted into wooden or bone hafts to form compound tools. Although few well-preserved specimens of such tools have survived to our times it is not difficult to ima-gine that they substantially extended the usefulness of stone implements, and by widening the working edge they overcame

34

their original clumsiness. Some of their raw materials were brought from far off; jaspers and cherts from settlements in the Ohře basin come from the Upper Palatinate and the striped chert found in North Bohemian sites from southern Poland. Various little blades of geometric shape (trapezoids, triangles, crescents, etc.), little round scrapers, burins, and many other small-size implements are typical of this stone industry.

Fig. 7

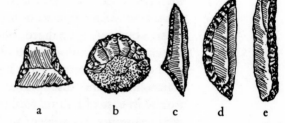

Fig. 7 Šakvice, S. Moravia. Meso-lithic microliths: (a) trapezium, (b) round-nosed scraper, (c) triangle, (d) segment, (e) retouched rectangular blade. 1:1

a   b   c   d   e

The oldest Mesolithic culture in Czechoslovakia, often compared to the West European Azilian culture, still shows many traditions of the Late Palaeolithic, but the later phases, the Sauveterrian and Tardenoisian, are already fully Mesolithic. The Tardenoisian sites in Bohemia, Moravia, and Slovakia form only a negligible part of the territorial diffusion of this culture reaching from West Europe as far as South Russia. North Moravia yielded finds belonging to the Świderian culture typical of the adjacent part of Poland. The cultural picture of this period is rather complicated and future excavations will hardly simplify it as it is a reflection of the advanced differentiation of the Mesolithic population in the whole of Europe.

CULTURE GROUPS

Not all the microliths referred to above were used for the manufacture of compound tools. Some of them, for instance the trapezoids, were arrow-heads as bow and arrow had in the meantime become generally adopted. Forest game of all sorts, from deer to little rodents, were hunted in this way and no doubt also snares and traps were set, although in the nature of things

HUNTING TECHNIQUES

35

we can never hope to find traces of them. The dog, which is generally assumed to have been domesticated at this period, participated in the chase.

FOOD

Already the fact that Mesolithic sites were usually situated on dunes in the neighbourhood of water or on the banks of rivers and lakes reveals that fishing must have been of great importance. Besides nets and baskets, so far not known in Czechoslovakia, fish-hooks of flint were used. Collected food included tortoises, snails, mussels, hazel-nuts, and acorns. On the whole, Mesolithic economy can be characterized as very intensive but not specialized, not restricted to only one source of sustenance but exploiting all of them. Thus the dependence on the herds of big animals that had been the sole source of food in Palaeolithic times disappeared, and with it the danger of catastrophe in case of failure. Only such an intensive and unspecialized economy combined with favourable conditions could lead to agriculture.

ECONOMIC
STRUCTURE

There is no doubt that the economy of the Mesolithic Age encouraged the natural division of labour. Food-collection must have been an even more important and reliable means of subsistence than the catch of the huntsmen and therefore the position of women in Mesolithic society was certainly one of consequence. It is most probable that the firm establishment of matriarchal clans fall into this period, but the sources in Czechoslovak territory do not give any clue in this respect.

SPIRITUAL
LIFE

So far very little is known about the spiritual life of Mesolithic man. His settlements are on sandy soils preserving only stones and no burials have yet been discovered. It is difficult to imagine that the art of the preceding period should have perished entirely. It is more probable that it was expressed in less durable materials (bone, wood, wicker-work, leather, etc.). It is necessary to keep in mind that Mesolithic sites, not only in Czechoslovakia but in the whole world, are extremely poor in objects of art. From Bohemia only very few traces of artistic feeling are known: a grooved pebble and mineral colours used evidently for the painting of bodies.

Scanty as our knowledge of the culture of Mesolithic man may be, we are yet able to recognize its most important contribution which lies in the sphere of economics—in the intensive exploitation of the natural surroundings which alone could have formed the basis for the advances of the following agricultural Neolithic period. As the natural conditions in Czechoslovakia were not favourable to such innovations the process leading to the Neolithic civilization did not take place there—the Mesolithic population of Central Europe got into a cul-de-sac and was absorbed by Neolithic agriculturalists coming from the south-east.

CHAPTER VI

The New Age: The Earliest Farmers

THE EARLY NEOLITHIC PERIOD: THE SECOND HALF OF THE
FIFTH AND FIRST HALF OF THE FOURTH MILLENNIUM B.C.

THE
NEOLITHIC
REVOLUTION

SINCE the rise of man the tool-maker there had been no such far-reaching changes in the sphere of economic life as those brought about by the Neolithic Age. While Palaeolithic and Mesolithic man lived in passive dependence on the forces of nature, Neolithic man exploited those forces to make them work to his own advantage. Man exerted himself only at the beginning and at the end of the process of production but the accumulation of food had become a controlled natural process —ears of corn as well as the bodies of animals. He began to change nature so that its processes ran in accordance with his own requirements. This entirely new attitude towards nature prepared by generations of Mesolithic populations was of enormous historic significance not only for the other branches of economy but potentially also for the organization of society and the manifestations of its spiritual life. That is why these changes are often called the Neolithic revolution. With this new way of life, nomadism was given up and the number of people finding subsistence in a certain area increased. Consequently the population rose from that of the Mesolithic period.

As already mentioned, natural conditions were not suitable for the origin of agriculture and stock-raising in Central Europe. The centre from which these innovations came was the area of the Eastern Mediterranean, with the Balkan peninsula and the Carpathian basin as subsidiary regions. In the earliest Neolithic period tribes of the so-called Starčevo culture (which was genetically connected with the Thessalian Sesklo-Dimini culture) populated these intermediary regions and underwent there a certain development, the last phase of which is called the Körös culture.

In Central Europe the earliest Neolithic culture was the Linear Bandkeramik of the Danube region. Formerly con, sidered quite independent, its genetic connexion with the Körös culture has recently been conclusively revealed. The oldest phase of Linear Bandkeramik ware springs directly from the Körös culture, taking over and continuing the shapes of the vessels (clay tubs, pedestalled bowls, globular pots, etc.), their orna, mentation (various lugs, the spiral, the so,called barbotine technique, etc.) as well as the way of working the clay and the surface. Traditions of the same culture can also be observed in other spheres as, for instance, in cult,objects (some idols, engra, vings on vessels) or in the polished stone implements and so on. In fact the resemblances are so marked that the genetic connexion of these two cultures must be admitted. But some elements of the oldest Linear Bandkeramik cannot be deduced from the Körös culture—we must attribute them to the influence of the Vinča culture which superseded the Starčevo,Körös culture in the southern regions of its diffusion.

ORIGIN OF THE LINEAR BANDKERAMIK

The development of the Linear Bandkeramik culture is clearly reflected in the alterations of the pottery; there were five distinct development phases. In this evolution we observe that the initial variety of shapes diminishes, gradually giving place to globular pots and simple bowls (so,called skeuomorphs). That is the reason why it took so long to trace their origin, as these apparent skeuomorphs had led to the erroneous derivation of pottery shapes from gourds. Well,formed bases and necks prevail during the earlier phases of this culture while in the later phases the vessels are mostly without flat bases and peculiar necks. The richness of ornamentation increases from phase to phase: in Bohemia the spiral (or volute), in Slovakia and Moravia the straight,lined patterns (nets, etc.) predominate. Excepting the

Plate 18

Plate 17

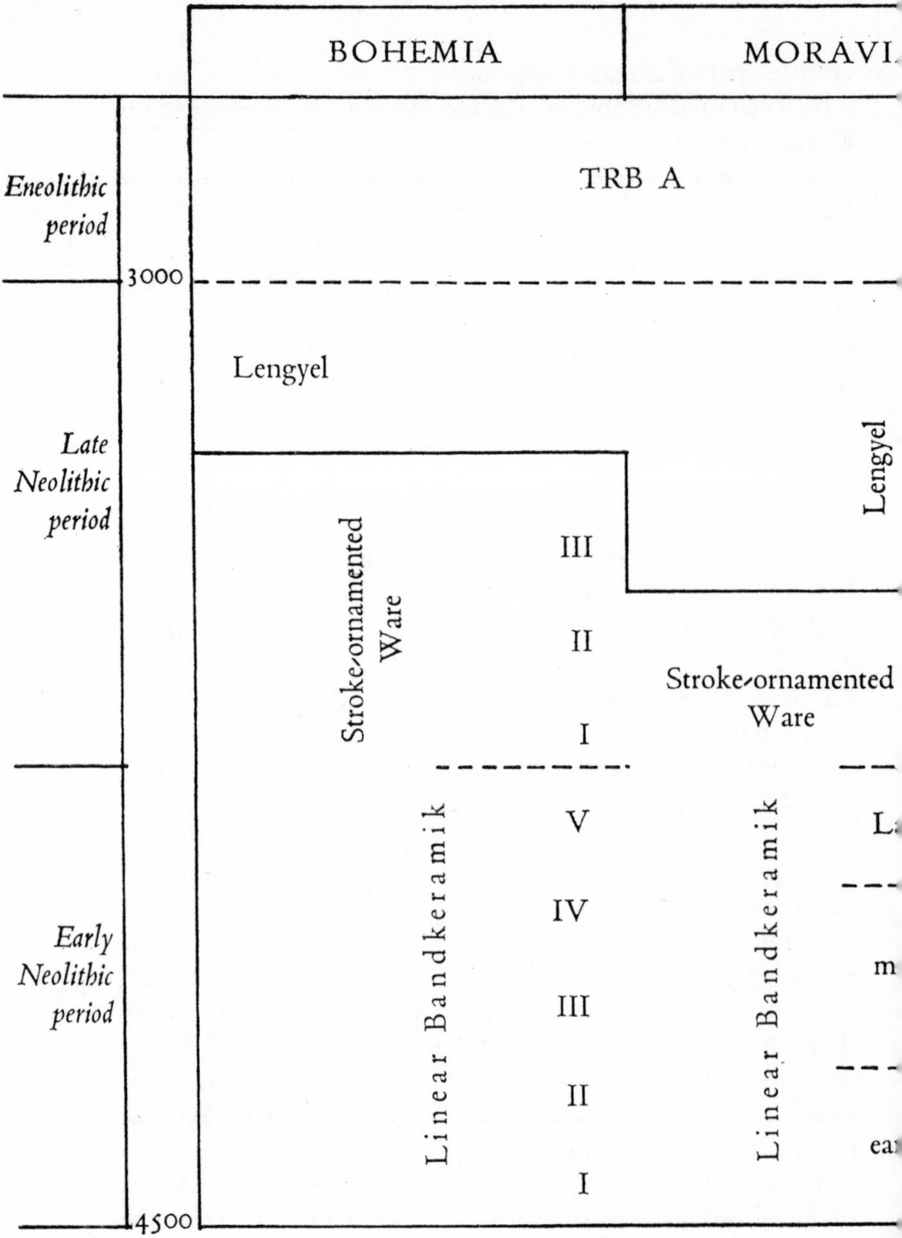

		BOHEMIA	MORAVI.

Eneolithic
period

3000

Late
Neolithic
period

Early
Neolithic
period

4500

TRB A

Lengyel

Lengyel

Stroke-ornamented
Ware

III

II

I

Stroke-ornamented
Ware

Linear Bandkeramik

V

IV

III

II

I

Linear Bandkeramik

L.

m

ea

Chart I   Tentative chronology o)

SOUTH-WEST SLOVAKIA	EAST SLOVAKIA
Ludanice	Tiszapolgár
Lengyel II Lengyel I	
Lužianky?	Tisza?
Železovce	Bükk
Linear Bandkeramik	East Slovakian Linear Pottery

olithic and Early Eneolithic in Czechoslovakia

earliest phase, the so-called musical note (*Notenkopf*) pattern continues from the beginning to the end and particularly so in the east.

The last phase of Linear Bandkeramik in Bohemia is called the Šárka type. Properly speaking it is a transitory phase leading to the culture of the Stroke Ornamented Ware. The two-fold tendency towards the simplification of shapes and multiplication of patterns culminates here, and instead of incised lines the application of rows of strokes characteristic of the succeeding Stroke Ornamented Ware, begins. In the Šárka type we meet also with the ware encrusted after firing which we know already in lesser numbers from the preceding phases.

THE
ŽELIEZOVCE
TYPE

At the time of the advance towards Stroke Ornamented Ware in Bohemia the development of the originally uniform culture of the Linear Pottery of South-West Slovakia took quite a different course. The incised lines continued there and their bundles were often crossed by long cuts. Also the painting (crusting) of vessels occurred very often. This late group, known under the term of Želiezovce type, did not develop any further; it was a dead branch of Linear Bandkeramik pottery.

EAST SLOVAK
LINEAR
POTTERY

In East Slovakia appeared a group differing to a considerable degree from that of the west. For the present this group is called East Slovak Linear Pottery and its content is not yet precisely known. It comprises high-pedestalled bowls as well as coarse vessels that remind one of the Körös culture from which it developed. In the ornamentation, which consists of wide grooves, appear typical wave-lines. It seems probable that further finds will enable us to establish a direct development from this East Slovak Linear Pottery to the succeeding Bükk culture.

THE BÜKK
CULTURE

The Bükk culture is mainly found in East Slovakia and the adjacent parts of Hungary but isolated examples of its pottery are also met with in South-West Slovakia and Moravia, and it even penetrated into southern Poland through the Carpathian mountain passes. The appearance of Bükk pottery in Moldavia is to be explained in the same way. It corresponds chronologically with the fourth to fifth phase of Linear Bandkeramik in the west and may partially overlap the Stroke Ornamented Ware. The Bükk culture, like others of that period, is characterized by a rich, particularly carefully-executed ornamentation of the vessels. The hemispheric bowls are covered all over with densely set incisions in the shape of Gothic arches, disintegrating spirals, and chessboard patterns. Settlements in caves as well as in the open air have survived. But the culture had no successors and led nowhere.

Plates 15, 21

We have seen how the Linear Bandkeramik groups, originally uniform, gradually disintegrated into local groups. One of them, the Šárka type in Bohemia was very important for the further development. From among the many local groups it was the only one that, in the following period, continued in the culture of the Stroke Ornamented Ware. Up to the present we do not know precisely the extent of the region of origin of this culture. It is certain that Central, and possible that North-West and East Bohemia belonged to it. From the Šárka type all the later pottery forms developed; shallow bowls, richly ornamented pear-shaped vessels, and globular pots with plastic decorations prevailed in the beginning, while later on beakers and other forms illustrating the influence of Lengyel Ware began to gain ground. The earlier examples are rich, the later plain; the earlier have vertical decoration, the later horizontal.

STROKE ORNAMENTED WARE

Plate 20

The Stroke Ornamented Pottery culture spread rapidly over considerable distances. The earlier phase occurs regularly in Bohemia, often in Moravia, even sometimes in South-West Slovakia: in the last-mentioned regions the late phases of the Stroke Ornamented Ware are always accompanied by Lengyel pottery. It has also been reported from Central and South Germany where the next stage of its development is known as the Rössen culture.

The situation in Slovakia at the time of the earliest phases of Stroke Ornamented Ware is not yet quite clear. It is poss, ible that some finds of Late Želiezovce Pottery, reported as associated with the earliest Stroke Ornamented Ware in South, West Slovakia, and of Late Bükk Ware from East Slovakia belong to this period. It seems probable, too, that we must assign to this period the sporadic and temporary diffusion of the Late Tisza culture not only in East but in South, West Slovakia as well. In the latter region the Tisza Ware was followed by the Lengyel culture, a late branch of the Vinča culture which arrived fully developed from the southern region of the Middle Danube.

Lengyel pottery also spread rapidly to South and East Moravia where its early forms appear at several sites in associa, tion with Late Stroke Ornamented Ware. It penetrated also into East Bohemia and from there it influenced the further development of the last phases of the Stroke Ornamented Ware in Central Bohemia and even farther west and north.

In the preceding description of the Neolithic period in Czechoslovakia we generally spoke in terms of cultures, not of peoples. To what degree does cultural radiation reflect the migrations of Neolithic farmers? Today archaeology and anthropology agree upon this issue, and we may take it for granted that the earliest agriculturalists were not the descendants of the native Mesolithic population but colonists from the south, east. Archaeology is able to prove that all the Central European Early Neolithic cultures were derived from the Körös culture and therefore closely related. Their differentiation, lasting at least one thousand years, certainly also coincided with the eth, nic differentiation of the originally uniform population. With the exception of spontaneous local developments in some regions the diffusion of the Stroke Ornamented Pottery culture can be taken as the reflection of a further wave of colonization covering the original, related Neolithic population. Another wave of immigrants belonging to the Lengyel culture gradually pushed the original Early Neolithic inhabitants towards the north-west, so that their coherent inhabitation ended in Central Bohemia with the end of the Stroke Ornamented Ware culture.

The mainstay of all the Early Neolithic cultures was agriculture, the details of which are not yet thoroughly known. The mobility of the settlements is generally explained by the slash-and-burn system which was certainly practised to some extent, but against its application to larger areas speaks the generally unchanged picture of the development of the forests as we know it from pollen diagrams. We may presume that the small-sized fields in the immediate vicinity of the settlements were worked with wooden implements and the crops harvested with wood or perhaps bone sickles mounted with flint blades. Nearly all the crops of cereal were cultivated: several kinds of wheat, barley, millet, and perhaps rye. Also leguminous plants, (peas, lentils, beans) were grown. The Early Neolithic inhabitation in Central Europe concentrated mainly on loess regions and only exceptionally on loam soils of the same fertility. This is the consequence of the specialization of the most ancient agriculture which, with its primitive equipment, dared not overstep the boundaries established by long experience. It also points to the fact that the proceeds were obviously so meagre that if any less fertile soil had been cultivated it would not have been sufficient to support life.

CROP-
RAISING

Our knowledge about stock-raising and hunting in this period is rather scanty as most of the settlements were situated on loess soils in which bones deteriorate rapidly. Besides the dog, cattle, sheep, goats, and pigs were kept but in what proportion is not yet known. Presumably the part played in economy by cattle-breeding was not an important one. Originally cows might not have been kept for meat at all but only for milk. This is suggested by the pottery strainers which were probably used in the production of cheese.

CATTLE-
BREEDING

HUNTING

Hunting is generally thought to have been of no importance among the activities of the Early Neolithic farmer. This opinion, however, may merely be the result of the generally poor condition of bones in the loess soils of the settlements: certainly from the Linear Pottery sites in Moldavia great quantities of bones of various animals have been reported. We may therefore presume that in Central Europe, too, hunting significantly supplemented the vegetable diet of the peasant. Already during the Bükk culture we know that deer (both red and roe), boar, and hares were hunted.

AGRICUL-
TURAL
IMPLEMENTS

The soil was tilled with wooden implements. The stone hoes, often mentioned in this connexion, were in reality adzes made for the working of wood. In general, adzes are characteristic of the Early Neolithic Age in Central Europe: mostly they appear in the shape of shoe-lasts, and are sometimes provided with perforations for handles. Stone maces were employed in later periods. From Neolithic sites a great number of polished stone tools is known: all of them were necessary not only for the construction of the large wooden houses but also to clear the forests for fields. The flaked stone industry (flint, chert, various quartzites) continued to exist side by side with the polished stone tools which were a Neolithic innovation. Associated with the oldest Linear Pottery occasionally a microlith industry appears, comprising mainly simple knives, end-scrapers and little blades with glossy cutting edges— accessories to sickles. Most typical of the various bone implements are the little chisels. Up to the present we do not know what weapons were used for hunting but it seems, by analogy with the related cultures of the Balkans, that the sling often served this purpose.

SETTLEMENTS

In Central Europe Neolithic settlements were generally located on the eastern slopes of loess elevations by the side of small expanses of water. Sometimes they were very extensive; for instance, at Bylany near Kutná Hora in Bohemia more

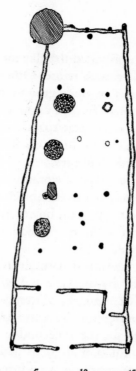

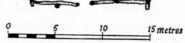

*Fig. 8 Postoloprty, N.W. Bohemia.
Ground plan of a long-house with entrance
and vestibule; inside, a row of dome-shaped
ovens. Stroke Ornamented Pottery culture*

than fifty large timber constructions have been brought to light
in the course of excavations which are still going on. Precise
determination of the actual extent and inner arrangement of
such settlements is prevented by the fact that most of them were
inhabited for a very long time, and probably even with inter-
ruptions, which makes it difficult to ascertain to which period
the individual buildings belonged. Houses up to forty metres
in length and six to eight metres wide are typical both of
the Linear Bandkeramik culture and the Stroke Ornamented
Ware. They consist of several rows of posts, the outer forming
the framework for wattle-and-daub walls, the inner supporting
the roof. Of these big buildings only post-holes and the traces
of furrows for the foundations remain, but associated with them
in several Neolithic settlements are a number of pits and hollows

Fig. 8

which provided the clay for the daubing of the walls and later got filled with refuse. Other pits may probably have served as granaries or underground store-rooms. Prehistoric settlements in Central Europe abound with such pits as the inhabitation spread over great spaces. Caves were also sometimes used as temporary dwellings in the time of the Linear Bandkeramik and Bükk cultures.

CLOTHING

A new type of clothing was among the Neolithic inventions —the use of woven fabrics made of wool, perhaps also of flax. Up to the present, however, very few whorls and loom weights belonging to the period of the Linear Pottery have been reported.

DIVISION OF LABOUR

A developed natural division of labour had been achieved already by the Late Palaeolithic and the Mesolithic Age. As time went on, the differences between hunting, cattle-breeding, and agriculture increased and with them the division of labour. While in the Palaeolithic and Mesolithic economies a great accumulation of goods had not been feasible or at least storing and preservation were impossible, in the Neolithic Age these obstacles no longer existed. Corn and cattle were sufficiently durable goods to allow accumulation. Gradually produce increased so far as to enable human society to nourish those who were not engaged in the production of food. Though several specialized occupations, for example the mining of lime-stone during the period of the Stroke Ornamented Ware, are established, it is not yet possible to see in it a higher type of division of labour or even a full-time specialization.

AGRICUL-TURAL SOCIETY

In the Neolithic Age people for the first time produced more goods than they needed. The accumulation of riches in itself, temporary and unreproducible as it was, could not yet immediately have caused a change in the society: the principal means of production, soil and cattle, were still owned in common; the people lived in large common dwellings and their food was prepared in communal ovens: at Bylany clusters of such ovens

48

have been found on the boundary of the village. The Neolithic revolution could have led to a new and differentiated society but it did not in fact do so until the productivity of agriculture and cattle-breeding had sufficiently increased and new forms of relations of production had been evolved.

Barter was the only method of commerce in the economy of the Neolithic Age. Raw materials, like obsidian, were traded directly over great distances, and barter which was carried on between clan and clan procured *Spondylus* shells and other luxuries.

BARTER

Plate 19

Although economic progress had already created the conditions for far-reaching social change, changes did not yet set in, as an alteration in the relations of production was slow to come. In the Neolithic Age, therefore, we meet with the same organization of society as in the preceding period. As it was woman's work—agriculture—that yielded the basic foods, the social standing of women must have risen considerably. Not only ethnographic analogies but also the female idols found in the settlements and the long, common dwellings (usually typical of societies at that stage of development), are indicative of matriarchy. These houses, known from many places in Czechoslovakia are evidence of a high degree of clan organization, as we know it from ethnographic descriptions of some North American tribes before the arrival of the European colonists.

MATRIARCHAL SOCIETY

Changes in Neolithic religion depended entirely on the changes in the economy and organization of society. There is no evidence that the Neolithic farmers worshipped individual deities, since in the society of that time the single individual did not play any important role. It is more probable that the oldest agriculturalists, in their dependence on the surrounding forces of nature, made them the objects of their worship. From the Linear Bandkeramik culture we know zoomorphic and anthropomorphic vessels of which some are provided with openings

RELIGION

for the pouring of liquids: there is no doubt that they were meant for use at the performance of religious rites. Their scarcity shows that these magic rites had developed so far as to be performed by a restricted group of persons only while the others watched. This differentiates them from most Palaeolithic rites in which all the members of the society actively took part. The new fashions in ritual were the pre-conditions for the formation of a special caste primarily con-cerned with the cult.

IDOLS

The Neolithic clay idols, which almost without exception represent women with the emphasis on sex, remain problema-tical. We can be certain that they were not goddesses but neither do other explanations answer the question satisfactorily. It seems most probable that they had been used as accessories to magic rites which must still have been widely practised in that period. In the recent Neolithic societies initiation rites formed an important part of the ritual—it is not impossible, therefore, that the Neolithic 'Venuses' served this purpose.

FUNERAL CULT

The funeral cult was little developed—in itself an indication of the small importance of the individual in the society of that time. This is reflected in the low number of known burials in relation to the number of settlements, in the poor equipment and simple construction of the graves as well as in the casual burials in settlement pits. The dead were buried in a contracted posi-tion in simple pits, sometimes strewn over with red ochre; and occasionally one vessel containing food, stone implements, or a spondylus shell were put into the grave. In the Stroke Orna-mented Ware culture cremation and inhumation were both practised, and already a greater number of vessels were provided. The two rites occur sometimes in the same cemetery which is the reason why it is so difficult to determine the significance of this difference. Cremation, which appears in Czechoslovakia for the first time in the Stroke Ornamented Ware culture, is evidence of a progressive conception of life hereafter, but, of course, it is difficult to recognize the religious ideas connected with it.

In contradistinction to the concrete religion of the Palaeolithic, the Neolithic cult is characterized by a developed symbolism. From the pictures on pottery objects especially we know many stylized symbols: crosses, swastikas, double-axes, and also schematized human figures. In South Slovakia, in the Domica cave, inhabited by people of the Bükk culture, were various designs drawn with burnt pine-wood, 'crown' patterns, etc. It does not seem impossible that the spiral also, one of the principal ornaments, was originally of symbolic significance. The origin, as well as the significance of some symbols is not yet clear, as, for instance, that of the double-axe which appears in a number of cults in the Eastern Mediterranean.

Religious symbolism and the abandonment of realism characterizes Early Neolithic art as it is expressed in clay figurines, in the strongly schematized bone idols (termed *spatulae*) derived from the Vinča culture, and particularly in the richly decorated pottery. On the vessels appear a great variety of ornamental systems and patterns of which many probably

SYMBOLISM

Fig. 9

DECORATIVE ART

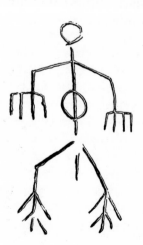

Fig. 9 Nová Ves, Central Bohemia. Human figure engraved on a Linear Bandkeramik storage-vessel. c. 1:3

51

originally had some symbolic significance which was later forgotten so that the mere ornament remained. To this category belong also some pattern of technical origin imitating, for instance, the protecting wicker-work or the wrapping of vessels. The oldest pottery was seldom decorated but if it was, then a pattern of individual lines adapted to the shape of the vessel covered its whole surface. In course of time the ornamentation became richer but was applied without any regard to the shape of the pot. Eventually the ornaments appear arranged in zones, the uppermost forming a ribbon under the rim. This style reached its peak at the end of the Linear and the beginning of the Stroke Ornamented Ware: after that time there is a remark-able drop in the number of decorated vessels accompanied by an improvement of their technological qualities.

The Neolithic Age brought a revolution in the sphere of production of material goods momentous by reason of its potentialities rather than its actual achievements. The relation between man and nature which was then established was to last until comparatively recent times. Yet there were so far no altera-tions in the forms of society; the economic changes, lacking intensity, did not disturb the social sphere. But the door to further developments was open.

CHAPTER VII

The New Wave of Farmers

IT was approximately at the period when the Linear Bandkera-mik originated in the north-western part of the Carpathian basin that farther to the south the earlier Starčevo culture was being superseded by the Vinča culture. The Lengyel culture like the Neolithic Boian, Gumelniţa, and Tripolye cultures, was a development of the Vinča culture. It began to branch off from the Vinča in the south of the Carpathian basin at about the same time as the peak period of Linear Pottery in the north. During the middle period of the Stroke Ornamented Ware culture, it expanded along the Danube to the north and occupied in its first phase South Slovakia, Lower Austria, and the southern part of Moravia, later penetrating also the south of Poland, Silesia, Bohemia, and South Germany. The situation in East Slovakia remains obscure in spite of the appearance of the Polgár culture which is certainly of Lengyel origin but belongs probably only in the Early Eneolithic period. In the northern and western marginal zones of the Central European inhabitation area late groups of Stroke Ornamented Ware competed with the Lengyel culture. Beyond these zones, in the north and in the west, mankind continued Mesolithic life.

ORIGIN OF
THE LENGYEL
CULTURE

The local group of the Lengyel culture which occupied South Moravia and South-West Slovakia is called Slovako-Moravian Encrusted (Painted) Ware. In contrast to the few forms of Late Linear Bandkeramik this culture is characterized by a wide variety of shapes, several types of bowls including pedestalled

LENGYEL
POTTERY

Plate 24

bowls, many types of beakers, pots (for example, clay tubs with six handles), and clay ladles. In the earliest phase their very rich decoration is incised and after the firing coated with red, yellow, or both; in the middle phase it is coated only in yellow or red, while in the late phase white prevails and finally incisions reappear.

ECONOMY

Probably cattle-breeding was more developed than in the preceding period although the animals that were domesticated remained the same. From the circumstance of the Lengyel culture, like its predecessor, being concentrated on loess soils and from the periodic mobility of its settlements one might draw the conclusion that the economic basis was similar.

IMPLEMENTS

Polished as well as chipped stone implements were still in general use. Copper was used only for ornaments not for tools. In the early phase obsidian from East Slovakia was often employed, but later its export to the west ceased. Most of the chipped implements were made of local raw materials. The axes were of slate as well as of hard rocks, some of them still of the shoe-last type, some with assymetrically ground cutting edges, others with pointed butts. Many axes appear perforated for hafts and a few, generally the smaller ones, have survived mounted on antler handles. In comparison with the Early Neolithic stone implements these specimens show the progress made by the Lengyel culture in tool-making. Besides stone, bone implements were used also, especially awls, chisels, and antler mace-heads, even fishing-hooks. The existence of a developed textile industry is proved only by a number of whorls found in the settlements as the many idols which occur unfortunately show no indication of clothes.

SETTLEMENTS

The Lengyel farmers located their settlements in the same places as their predecessors with Linear Bandkeramik, mostly on the eastern slopes of loess elevations, though settlements under over-hanging rocks and in caves are also known.

Plate 22

Some of them as, for instance, Hluboké Mašůvky in South

Moravia, were enclosed by a ditch. At Hluboké Mašůvky the longer diameter of the enclosed area measured 350 metres. The ditches, not very deep or wide (maximum 2·80 metres and 4·50 metres), were interrupted by many causeways, and some were provided with wood gates placed before the line of ditches. These gates are reminiscent of Balkan stone architec‑ture but considering their imperfect construction they can hardly ever have been of any practical value in Central Europe. The ditch enclosures are the predecessors of similar earthworks of the Michelsberg culture in Western Germany and the same traditions are recognizable again as far afield as the English Windmill Hill culture.

So far very few houses have been excavated, but that they were timber constructions of rectangular outline we know not only from their ground‑plans but also from a clay model from

Fig. 10

Fig. 10 Střelice. Clay model of a hut. Moravian painted ware. c. 1 : 2

Střelice in Moravia. Wattle-and-daub walls connected the peripheral posts, as seen in the model, and the hut was covered with a span roof at the top of which a bull's head was placed above the open front. Some other models show a dwelling with an ante-room as in the twenty-metre-long hut at Klučov (East Bohemia). Most of the settlement finds come from the pits which were quite a common feature there.

SOCIAL
STRUCTURE

The Lengyel culture represents a matured Neolithic group with a rich cultural tradition. The contrast between settlements with ditched enclosures and settlements without them is indicative of an intricate social structure. From cult characteristics (female idols) a further development of matriarchy is generally inferred but it is necessary to keep in mind that signs suggestive of the rite of suttee (double burials of a man and woman), a feature of matured patriarchy, have also been reported.

Fig. 11

Among the cult-objects at our disposal are anthropomorphic and zoomorphic vessels, and animal and human idols of baked clay. The vessels in the shape of stylized animals (bull, pig) probably contained liquids required at the performance of religious rites. Usually the anthropomorphic vessels do not represent whole figures but only parts of them as, for instance, that from Svodín in Slovakia: human arms bent at the elbows project upwards from a globular body, otherwise only the nipples and perhaps the ears are represented by means of protuberances. Most numerous are beakers in the form of human legs. A remarkable vessel was found at Střelice near Znojmo in Moravia. On this object four double rhomboids (? female sex) alternate with four human figures of which three are similar, and have two legs (? men) while the fourth figure has only one, pedestal-like leg (? woman in skirt). The designs are executed in strokes encrusted with white. Statuettes of animals, probably also used at magic rites, appear in abundance in Lengyel settlements and represent horned cattle, goats, sheep (rams), dogs, ducks, and fish. In the same class belong pottery

Fig. 11 Výčapy-Opatovce, S.W. Slovakia. Burial of a man and woman. Lengyel culture. 1 : 25

handles or lugs in the shape of animals. They show us which species man of the Late Neolithic Age was interested in and wanted to influence through magic. For the purposes of magic their images had to be true. This did not exclude conventional stylization but it required the representation of real, existing animals; it is only seldom that we meet with figurines of double-headed goats or a two-headed bull on a clay lid.

In the anthropomorphic plastic art we find female figurines sometimes standing, or rarely sitting, with the emphasis on the sexual features. The figures are conventionally stylized and the position of the arms is sometimes regarded as a gesture of adoration. Generally the arms are represented by stumps only, and the details of the head not elaborated. Most of these figurines are middling sized (fifteen to twenty centimetres) but some are thirty-five centimetres tall, and their number in Lengyel settlements is remarkable. They appear not to have been treated very carefully as most of them have been found in fragments even when associated vessels have been in a better state of preservation. It is most improbable that at this stage of economic and social development anthropomorphic gods should have been known, and more likely these idols, like the similar ones of the Linear culture, were magic figurines used at the performance of initiation ceremonies.

LENGYEL
IDOLS

Plate 26

It is by no means impossible that already in the Lengyel period the cult of the axe, known from the succeeding Eneolithic era, was practised. Clay imitations of stone battle-axes, perhaps also ritual objects, would suggest it.

Funeral customs were not more developed than they had been in the culture with the Linear Pottery. Considering the number of settlements, remarkably few burials are known. Besides casual burials in settlements the inhumation rite in the contracted position and the cremation rite were practised. From Slovakia we know of a greater number of graves, some with several vessels, but from Moravia very few. At Džbánice

BURIAL
CUSTOMS

Plate 23

in Moravia twelve skeletons, the skull of a dog, and fourteen vessels were squeezed into a pit with a diameter of 2·5 metres— but such a burial is unique. From several places evidence of cannibalism has been reported: human bones with traces of incisions in association with animal bones. These cases of anthropophagy must have had a ritual character as by that time there would have been plenty of other kinds of food available.

THE FIRST
INDO-
EUROPEANS

The Lengyel culture was of enormous importance for the further destiny of Central Europe. Though not properly of Middle European origin it gave rise to the TRB culture (or Funnel-necked Beakers), the local development of it in this region. There is a continuous development from the TRB people to the historic Illyrian, Celtic, Teutonic, Baltic, Slavonic and perhaps even the Italian nations. Later on we shall see that the expansion of the people with the Lengyel culture was the last great prehistoric invasion of Central Europe, the last possibility for the immigration of Indo-European tribes. Of course, the Lengyel culture must have represented already differentiated Indo-Europeans dispersing later into many language groups, of which only a few have continued to form the nucleus of the known historic nations.

CHAPTER VIII

The Advanced Farmers of the Eneolithic Period

BEGINNINGS OF PATRIARCHAL SOCIETY
THE THIRD AND EARLY SECOND MILLENIUM B.C.

IN Czechoslovakia as well as in the whole of Central Europe the Eneolithic period was of long duration and great import-ance. This era laid the foundations of further social develop-ment. Although copper had already appeared sporadically by that time, it does not seem justified to choose it as a key-term for the definition of this epoch as, thus far, the economic import-ance of metal had been negligible. Other economic, social, and cultural phenomena characterize it much better.

THE EARLY ENEOLITHIC PERIOD

In Czechoslovakia the history of the Eneolithic period begins with the emergence of the culture producing Funnel-necked Beakers (TRB culture) which, in its earliest phase, spread rapidly over the vast area of Central Europe. It significantly influenced South Scandinavia, and also to some extent West Europe, where contemporary groups, such as the Michelsberg or the Windmill Hill cultures, are considered as still Neolithic. Up to the present its origin has remained obscure, save that we know that this must be looked for in Central Europe somewhere in the sphere of the Late Lengyel groups.

ORIGIN OF THE TRB CULTURE

In Slovakia the survival of the Lengyel groups into the Early Eneolithic Age can be taken for granted. From the Late

METALLURGY IN SLOVAKIA

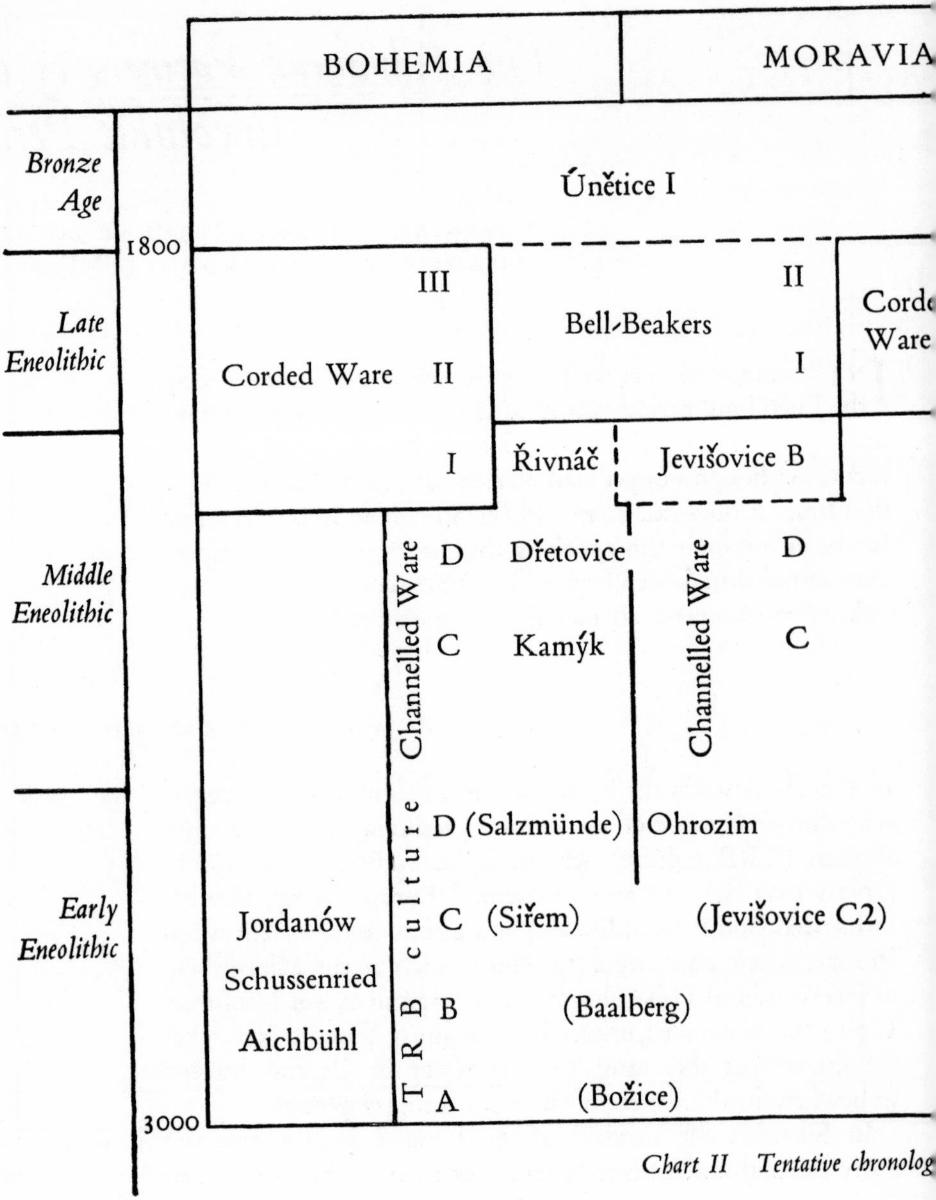

	BOHEMIA	MORAVIA

		BOHEMIA	MORAVIA
Bronze Age		Únětice I	
	1800		
Late Eneolithic		Corded Ware III II I	Bell-Beakers II I	Corded Ware
		Řivnáč	Jevišovice B
Middle Eneolithic		Channelled Ware D Dřetovice C Kamýk	Channelled Ware D C
Early Eneolithic		Jordanów Schussenried Aichbühl	TRB culture D (Salzmünde) Ohrozim C (Siřem) (Jevišovice C2) B (Baalberg) A (Božice)
	3000		

Chart II Tentative chronolog

	SOUTH-WEST SLOVAKIA		EAST SLOVAKIA
Mierzanowice			
I I	Nagyrév I (Čaka)		
(Bošáca)		Channelled Ware E	Channelled Ware
		Channelled Ware D	
	(Úny)	Channelled Ware C	
	(Fonyód)	Channelled Ware B	
	(Boleráz)	Channelled Ware A	
	Bodrogkeresztúr ?		Bodrogkeresztúr
	Ludanice		Tiszapolgár

Eneolithic and Early Bronze Age in Czechoslovakia

Lengyel culture in South-West Slovakia the Ludanice group developed and in the east the Polgár culture with its succeeding stage, the Bodrogkeresztúr culture. These cultures, especially the two last mentioned attained a considerable prosperity. The astonishing maturity of their metallurgy is attested by the burials of the cemetery at Tibava in East Slovakia. Here almost every grave contained a copper axe-adze made of ore from Central Slovakian deposits as well as scores of vessels. These Slovak cultures, however, represent dead branches of the development, since they were all later absorbed by the culture with the Channelled Ware.

THE DEVELOP-
MENT OF THE
TRB CULTURE

On the basis of ceramic objects four phases, labelled A–D, can be recognized in the development of the TRB culture. The characteristic typology of phase A, so far represented only by some finds from Moravia and Bohemia, is important, since as a manifestation of the early expansion of TRB culture it is almost identical throughout the whole territory of Central Europe and South Scandinavia. Richness and variety of shape distinguish the Moravian finds—comprising not only funnel-necked beakers but also amphorae with a number of lugs at the lower part of the body, two-handled amphorae, jugs, and a pedestalled bowl—from their northern analogies.

Phase B is represented by the Baalberg group. Its territorial extent, reaching from Central Germany to Poland, Bohemia, and Moravia, though still great, appears somewhat reduced. In this phase a strict profilation is characteristic of the ceramics which include again funnel-necked beakers, now taller and slimmer; two- and four-handled, funnel-necked amphorae sometimes also with four handles at the biggest extension of the body; jugs with the handle at half the height of the funnel-shaped neck; and many other forms, especially bowls and pots with a plastic ribbon under the rim.

In phase C we meet in Bohemia with the Siřem group and in Moravia with the Jevišovice group (stratum C2) both of which

Plate 28

Fig. 12

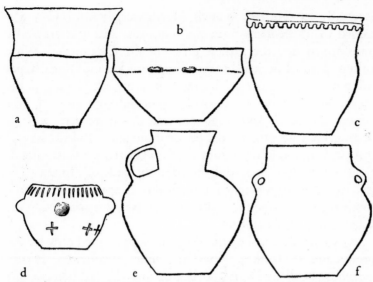

Fig. 12 Pottery of the TRB culture: (a) and (c) funnel-necked beakers, (b) bowl, (d) miniature vase, (e) jug of the Baalberg type, (f) amphora. Střelice (c), Jevišovice (S.W. Moravia) (a, b, d, f) and Němčice (N. Moravia) (e). 1 :5

have many analogies in Poland. In this period the ceramic objects are ornamented with stamped patterns which had originally been crusted. The shape of the funnel-necked beakers approaches that of bowls and the jugs have ribbon handles projecting from the rim.

Phase C led to phase D represented by the Salzmünde group in Bohemia and the Ohrozim group in Moravia. Now the differences between Bohemia and Moravia were already considerable and the development here splits distinctly into two lines. The Salzmünde group is characterized by pottery of a looser profilation with a decoration derived from the Siřem group from which it had developed. Once developed it expanded from Central Bohemia in a north-western direction and reached Central Germany. The Ohrozim group in Moravia,

especially its southern branch (Jevišovice, stratum C1) absorbed many elements from the south-east and was gradually
transformed into the earliest phase of the Channelled Ware
culture. Funnel-necked beakers of more or less indistinct shapes
still often occur in the north but, as it seems, are lacking in the
south. Jugs and bowls are richly decorated with grooves, and
almost biconical amphorae are often ornamented with a
herring-bone pattern. Under the denomination 'Boleráz group'
this phase is also known from Lower Austria, the Burgenland,
South-West Slovakia, and the adjacent parts of Hungary. In
isolated cases it penetrated into South Germany, and to the
south it got almost to the Adriatic Sea; there it is assigned to the
Channelled Ware culture.

TOOLS   As we have seen, the knowledge of copper, used only for the
production of trinkets (bracelets, little ornaments), luxury
weapons (battle-axes) and rarely axes or awls, had been, so far,
of no economic importance. At that time stone was still the
commonly used raw material for tools. The axes we know are
of ground stone and only exceptionally of flint with symmetrical
edges. Imported stone, especially from Poland, was used as well
as local. Bones were again often employed, particularly for the
manufacture of awls and chisels; hoes made of antler were
probably more effective than the earlier variety made of wood.

TEXTILES   Obviously the textile industry must have reached a high
degree of accomplishment as hundreds of whorls, many
decorated, have been found in the settlements of this period.

POTTERY   The ceramic production is characterized by shapes approaching the maximum of perfection obtainable without the knowledge of the potter's wheel. The difference between the coarse
ware for the storing or preparation of food and the table vessels
appears definitely established. Apart from a few insignificant
changes the repertory of shapes comprising simple pots,
beakers, cups, bowls, jugs, and amphorae remains the same
from the TRB culture until the Late Hallstatt period.

The changes in the sphere of agriculture are less apparent in   AGRICULTURE
the Early Eneolithic Age than in the succeeding Middle
Eneolithic period. But we must suppose that the importance of
cattle-breeding and hunting rose as agricultural production
increased. This does not at all mean a return to Mesolithic
traditions which, after at least a thousand years of Neolithic
development, were now entirely superseded on the fertile soils
of Central Europe. Especially for the last phases the first use
of ploughing implements drawn by horned cattle can be
supposed. Besides an improved agriculture, cattle-breeding
and hunting, food-gathering, particularly of river mussels, is
documented. Wild garlic was eaten for its taste and curative
effects.

Economic changes were now sufficiently pronounced to   PATRIARCHAL SOCIETY
cause far-reaching social changes. It seems that the new division
of labour shifted to the foreground men who could sometimes acquire considerable wealth. Impressive graves for
single individuals bear witness to the fact that the stratification
of society had already begun—it was certainly not within every-
body's reach to get interred in a grave like the Nordic dolmens,
the tombs of the Polish Kujawish type, or the Moravian long
barrows. In this period also we meet with the first specialized
fighting weapons, stone battle-axes. In former periods the same
weapons had served for both hunting and fighting. But the
Early Eneolithic seems to have been a time of pronounced
martial development, doubtless accompanied by the creation of
those patriarchal families which are found fully established in
the following Middle Eneolithic period. It is significant that
besides settlements in lowlands we now also find communities
established on barely accessible hill-tops, which reflects rather
unrest at home and clan fights of a differentiating society than
an invasion by foreigners.

While in the Lengyel culture certain signs in the sphere of   CULT-OBJECTS
cult possibly explicable as traces of matriarchy or of its survial

could be found, nothing of this kind is met with in the TRB culture.

In the earlier phases cult-objects are relatively rare. From phases C and D we know zoomorphic vessels covered with symbolic signs (crosses, etc.) which occur also on other objects. Like the clay drums from these phases they may have served ritual purposes. In phase D female idols appear again, but in lesser numbers than before; they are strongly schematized and, as seen later on, represent probably anthropomorphic deity. The miniature battle-axes in clay from the settlements of the TRB culture in Bohemia and Moravia show that the cult of the axe was at that time widely diffused in Europe.

BURIAL
CUSTOMS

Although we do not yet know of any graves from the oldest phase of the TRB culture in Czechoslovak territory, we may suppose that the custom of burying at least some of the dead in regular graves was already firmly established in the Eneolithic Age. Though often restricted to the chieftains, graves are a common phenomenon in the Baalberg group (phase B) and in all the later phases. During the TRB culture grave goods are rare (usually only a jug or an amphora) and the superior standing of the dead man can be inferred only from the size and complication of the funerary architecture. But settlement burials belonging to less distinguished members of the patri-archal families are also known. In Bohemia and Moravia graves from the Baalberg group were still simple (in the soil or in stone cists) but already those from the Salzmünde group (phase D) were covered with barrows. From both these groups we know contracted skeleton burials while those belonging to the Ohrozim group in North Moravia are cremation burials, several of them under long and narrow barrows (up to the length of twenty-one metres). The ashes were in simple pots, sometimes provided with a hole (*Seelenloch*) for the soul of the deceased, and accompanied by vessels. The whole shape and the details of the construction of the barrows indicate the southernmost projection of the Nordic megalithic graves adapted to the Moravian milieu of the TRB culture.

Besides the TRB culture there existed in Bohemia a number of other Eneolithic cultures of western origin. The oldest of these is the Aichbühl culture, a Late Lengyel group which penetrated from South Germany into the region of Plzeň. The next stage in its development, the Schussenried culture, characterized by richly ornamented jugs, is already met with in the whole of Bohemia. In the course of phase C of the TRB culture the Jordanów (Jordansmühl) culture developed here from the Schussenried and expanded as far as Silesia. We do not know of any settlements from this culture but the sherds of its fine wares are found in the settlements of phase C of the TRB culture, and the graves of this period, rather rich, belong to the Jordanów culture. In Jordanów burials there appear ceramic forms with details which are reminiscent of Lengyel tradition, but to label the Jordanów as a Late Lengyel group does not seem appropriate.

Also of western origin is the Michelsberg culture, whose classic forms are known from Western Germany and the Low Countries. In Bohemia, tulip-shaped beakers and bowls with inverted rims are typical of it.

THE MIDDLE ENEOLITHIC AGE

As has already been said, the Channelled Ware culture had its origin in phase C of the TRB culture in South Moravia and the adjoining regions. It was a direct development, but influences from the south-east, among them chanelling and some other types of ornament contributed. From its native region Channelled Ware expanded rapidly west to Bohemia and the Swiss frontier, north to the region of Kuyaria, and south-east to the Carpathian basin and beyond

Fig. 13

Plate 33

into Serbia and Rumania. In the Carpathian basin especially the diffusion of this culture represents a real ethnic expansion absorbing the native population of the Late Lengyel phases (Bodrogkeresztúr culture).

In its native region the culture producing Channelled Ware can be divided into five phases which we mark with the letters A–E. The earliest phase is represented by the contents of stratum C1 of the significant site of Jevišovice in South Moravia. This approaches the TRB culture very closely but the characteristic beakers themselves are lacking in it. The Boleráz type in which signs of the TRB culture are even rarer forms an almost identical group in South-West Slovakia. Phase B repre- sents the transition to the so-called Baden pottery (phase C) which used to be thought earlier and typical of Channelled Ware. The end of Channelled Ware is formed by phases D and E. The last phase no longer occupies the whole territory: in East Moravia and South-West Slovakia it is represented by the Bošáca group which already differs considerably from the original culture. Just as with the preceding cultures, after an original uniform expansion, a number of phases developed in which the culture with Channelled Ware disintegrated into smaller groups. But not all of them formed the bases for further developments.

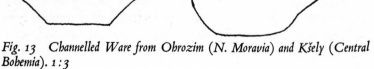

Fig. 13   Channelled Ware from Ohrozim (N. Moravia) and Kšely (Central Bohemia). 1:3

We left Bohemia in the Salzmünde (D) phase of the TRB culture. The further development is not quite clear as it is not until phase C of the Channelled Ware that we meet here the so called Kamýk group, which has both similarities to and differences from the Baden pottery. The next development of this Bohemian group led to phase D, characterized by the rich burial at Velvary. The large stone cist of this grave contained, besides perfectly shaped pottery, an ornamented gorget of copper sheet, spiral bracelets of copper, shells and their imitations in copper—altogether, indeed, a splendid outfit for this period.

The further development of this Bohemian Channelled Ware brings us to the Řivnáč culture which is characteristic of the end of the Middle Eneolithic Age in Bohemia. This culture not only represents the traditions of the Channelled Ware but shows also new elements of northern origin. It is probable that even in the preceding phase the Globular Amphorae culture which originated in Poland from the local group of the TRB culture had already infiltrated into Bohemia from Central Germany. Besides the so-called 'western group' from Germany, frequently met with in Central Bohemia, a Silesian group of Globular Amphorae also expanded towards the south to North Moravia and East Bohemia. Both seem to have co-existed with the Řivnáč culture. Graves belonging to the Řivnáč culture are very rare, but quite a number of rich burials of the Globular Amphorae culture are known in Bohemia. On the other hand, the Globular Amphorae culture has neither independent settlements nor any coarse pottery: its table wares are found in the sites belonging to the Řivnáč culture. This fact is suggestive of a probable domination of the native population with the Řivnáč culture by the Globular Amphorae people.

Besides these elements from the Channelled Ware and Globular Amphorae cultures we also find in the Řivnáč culture other elements. First there are the so-called Bernburg cups,

THE ŘIVNÁČ
CULTURE AND
GLOBULAR
AMPHORAE

Plate 32

69

probably taken over by the western (German) group of the Globular Amphorae during their passage through Central Germany and brought by them to Bohemia. The so-called Ljubljana marsh (Ljubljansko barje, Laibacher Moor) bowls, decorative, small, and pedestalled, represent an isolated element taken over from the region of the Eastern Alps through the intermediary of the Moravian Jevišovice culture.

THE
JEVIŠOVICE
CULTURE

In phase E the development of the culture with Channelled Ware continues in the Bošáca group in East Moravia and Slovakia. At that time we meet in South-West Moravia with the rather different Jevišovice culture (Jevišovice, stratum B) which closely resembles the Bohemian Řivnáč culture, but without the elements from the Globular Amphorae which did not penetrate so far to the south. Instead, there was a strong southern influence from the sphere of the Ljubljana marsh.

Finally it is necessary to mention that the earliest phase of the Corded Ware culture also falls into these later phases of the Middle Eneolithic period in Bohemia. So far, however, no finds directly connecting it with the domestic development have been reported.

IMPLEMENTS

The stone industry continues although the relative importance of stone implements diminished. Great polished axes with symmetrical cutting edges as well as little wedges with only one ground edge, were widely used. Hammer-axes with haft perforations are common. Metal implements were more often used than in the previous period, as is shown by the hoard from Brno-Líšeň containing a set of copper tools for the working of wood, but one must not overestimate their importance in the contemporary economy. Bone and antler tools, especially antler hoes were still often employed.

The ceramic objects, technically of high standard, show a great variety of shapes. Plain pots with an applied ribbon under the rim and a roughened body are most common. Jugs and dippers with ribbon handles reaching far above their rims are particularly typical of the groups with Channelled Ware. A prominent place in the Bohemian group with Channelled Ware and especially in the Řivnáč culture is taken by jugs with horned handles (*ansa cornuta*), whose particular significance will be discussed later, and by the beautifully decorated pottery of the Globular Amphorae culture.

Fig. 14

As already mentioned, from the Eneolithic Age on, a new quite particular group of objects, weapons specifically intended for fighting, appears. The battle-axe is now joined by the copper dagger, the numbers of which rise substantially in the Bell-Beaker culture only. Bone arrow-heads are typical of the Řivnáč culture while other contemporary groups used flint.

SPECIALIZED WEAPONS

We were only able to conjecture the cause of the prosperity of the TRB culture, but for the Middle Eneolithic period we possess reliable material evidence. A movement to light sandy soils, probably stimulated by the use of ploughing implements which can be safely assumed for all this period, can be observed all over Central Europe. But cattle-breeding, food-gathering, and fishing were also carried on, as we know from the bones found in their settlements. We may therefore assert that the economy of the Eneolithic Age was highly effective, and that it represented the perfect adaptation of the Central European population to their natural surroundings.

PLOUGHING

Such far-reaching changes in economy caused a very rapid development of the social organization. In discussing the preceding Early Eneolithic period, in which these changes began, we were sometimes faced with alternatives, but in the Middle Eneolithic period plenty of safely interpretable finds enable us to reach firm conclusions. As is proved by some burials in adjacent countries (Central Germany and Poland) the new economy was tied to the natural division of labour. Cattle, ploughing, and the cultivation of the fields were no longer the domain of women. It was now the men who produced the necessities of life, and the women were left with

CHANGE TO A PATRIARCHAL SOCIETY

71

Fig. 14 Small jug, with ansa cornuta. *Řivnáč culture. Praha-Ďáblice. c. 1:6*

domestic work like the preparation of food, and the production of textiles or of pottery. In the Neolithic period both the sexes had participated equally in the maintenance of the whole— sometimes woman's share was the bigger one—but now the system of patriarchal families emerges in which women play a subordinate role while men have the power. This power of man over his family was so great that his wife, and sometimes all his family, were slain, to accompany him to the other world. This custom, termed 'suttee', resulted in a considerable decimation of the population and was therefore restricted to men of distinction.

Ploughing had by now probably increased the productivity of human work to such a degree that the single individual was able to produce more food than was necessary to cover his immediate needs. A situation was thus created in which one member of society could take advantage of the work of another man and keep the surplus for himself. Cattle were already private property; the new economic system meant that those who did not own beasts of draught could not plough, and were therefore at an extreme disadvantage compared with those who could. Material evidence from Central Europe proves that the development did actually take place. The members of a patriarchal family no longer all enjoyed equal rights; they were ruled by the head of the family. In the preceding chapter we mentioned that the fundamental preconditions of a differentiation of society had been formed in the Neolithic Age but that the production of material goods had not yet attained sufficient intensity to change the interrelations of production and the organization of society depending on them. This decisive intensity of production was reached in the Eneolithic Age, but it was still not strong enough to provoke any deeper division of society.

FORTIFIED SETTLEMENTS

We know from the general reduction in the size of the settlements at that time that the patriarchal family had now become the economic unit. It could hardly have exceeded the Plate 29 number of fifty persons in one generation. The period of the great Neolithic villages was over. The settlements very often occupy places protected by nature, like hill-tops, and are even fortified. The settlement on the Homolka hill near Kladno in Plate 30 Central Bohemia has been systematically excavated. Two lines of fortification, consisting of palisades with two gates belonging to two settlement phases, could be identified. In the earlier phase this settlement contained about six houses, in the later phase at least ten. Consequently the number of persons living there simultaneously could never have been very great and corresponds with our conception of one to three large patriarchal families. Hill-top settlements are particularly typical of the Řivnáč culture of which the people with Globular Amphorae are the leading representatives. As mentioned before, these martial measures reflect fights among the social units of this culture rather than the need for defence against an invasion from abroad (usually one thinks here of the Corded Ware culture).

There is a further change in the character of the cult. In this RITUAL period the performance of rites is definitely transferred to a specialized person, probably to the head of the patriarchal family who, through the cult, exerts influence on the other members of his family. This is reflected in the rich graves with clay drums and in a hut of the Řivnáč settlement at Vraný in Plate 31 Central Bohemia where an idol and a drum have been found together.

The idols from this period are strongly schematized and some types represent unreal, fantastic beings. To this category belong the so-called horned idols which have animal horns instead of heads. The horned idols and the *ansa cornuta* handles appertain to the Channelled Ware culture; in the Bohemian line they are more numerous and characteristic; and in the Řivnáč culture their number is uncommonly great. In Moravia and in Slovakia only simple forms of the *ansa cornuta* are met with. From the

Fig. 15 Horned idol of the Řivnáč culture. Homolka hill-fort, Central Bohemia.
c. *1 : 1*

Jevišovice culture in Moravia we know highly stylized stone idols which possibly represent a two-headed deity. Horned idols from Bohemia imitating patterns from the Gumelniţa culture in the Balkans illustrate the variety and oddity of the cult-forms in this period. Analogies from abroad show that in the Middle Eneolithic period the conception of anthropomor-phic deities must have taken its origin. This is quite compre-hensible considering how the status and sphere of activities of the single individual, in whose image the first deities were made, were extended during this period. Therefore we can infer that the Eneolithic idols represent real gods.

Though relatively rare, the burials of the Middle Eneolithic period are often ostentatious and some of them are of such an exceptional character that they cannot have belonged to the common members of society (for example, that at Velvary). The interments of the Channelled Ware culture are mostly cremation burials but from Czechoslovakia we do not know any cemeteries as important as from neighbouring Hungary. The cremation cist grave from the Řivnáč culture at Stehelčeves near Kladno in Central Bohemia contained, besides pottery, a strongly stylized stone idol but this is exceptional in an inter-ment. In the culture associated with Globular Amphorae the dead are always buried as inhumations. Most of the con-tracted skeletons are interred in the soil and provided with several vessels and a pig's jaw, obviously representing a special delicacy. The grave furniture may also often contain a clay drum indicative of the particular standing of the deceased, or four human skulls placed in the corners of the cist as at Před-měřice in East Bohemia.

Since there are few cult-objects, art did not find any particular application except in the ornamentation of pottery, which seems to have been purely decorative. Characteristic of this decoration is the contrast between light and shade achieved by the channelling of the vessels and by deeply impressed patterns.

For Central Europe and consequently also for Czecho-slovakia the Early and Middle Eneolithic Age is of particular significance. It is the period when cultures coming from the south-east for the first time perfectly adapted themselves to their Central European natural surroundings. At that time the differentiation of prehistoric society appears firmly established. The patriarchal organization no longer allows the equality of all its members and the forms in which this inequality manifested itself were often cruel. The basis of the patriarchal family was the private ownership of the means of production, draught animals and ploughing implements. But side by side with it the common ownership of land continued to exist and the traditions of the preceding periods were still strong. Social differentiation had not yet created special groups but led only to the periodic rise of single individuals from the original equality of the collective group.

THE LATE ENEOLITHIC AGE

As mentioned above, in the northern part of Central Europe the development of the late groups of the TRB culture took a somewhat different course. Somewhere in the wider region of the Lower Vistula the new Globular Amphorae culture developed gradually from phase D of the TRB culture Wiórek group. This group spread rapidly to the east as far as the Middle Dnieper and towards the west to East Germany and Bohemia, where it helped to form the Řivnáč culture. Generally the expansion of the Globular Amphorae culture represents ethnic movements.

Several local groups of the eastern line of this culture evolved into the Corded Ware culture. The transition was not the result of any foreign influences. It can be well observed in Little Poland where from the Late Globular Amphorae the so-called Złota culture, a group within the Corded Ware cul-ture, developed, and also in the north where we find on the shores of the Baltic Sea a similar group called the Rzucewo arising from similar roots. It seems that there were other late groups of the Globular Amphorae that had an analogous development towards the Corded Ware culture but only a few of them expanded over the whole of Central, North, and East Europe. The Danish and Swedish Battle-axe cultures and the pit-graves with ochre-covered skeletons in the north of the Black Sea region are all probably consequences of this powerful expansion. In the vast areas of Europe the earliest phase of the culture with Corded Ware is of remarkable typological uni-formity and the funerary rite is also the same—evidences of the rapid ethnic expansion of the Corded Ware people.

CORDED
WARE IN
BOHEMIA AND
MORAVIA

In Czechoslovakia, Bohemia and Moravia were overrun by the people with the Corded Ware. In the very first period Bohemia was invaded from the north, up the river Elbe. It was not until later that the less important wave from Lusatia to the region of the Upper Elbe joined this movement. Up to the present we know nothing of the earliest phase in Moravia, and indeed very little of the middle phase; most of the finds belong to the latest phase and show northern connexions, especially with Silesia. Of course, the infiltration of the Corded Ware culture from Bohemia into Moravia is possible.

Fig. 16

Plate 34

The development of the Corded Ware culture in Bohemia is well known. The earliest horizon (I), common to the whole of Central Europe, is characterized by beakers with funnel-shaped necks and amphorae with decorations in metopes, accompanied by elegant battle-axes of the so-called Pan-European type. Up till now there have been no finds containing all these objects. The first phase of the culture with Corded Ware was perhaps still contemporary with the Řivnáč culture.

The middle phase consists partly of a continuation of the previous one (the group termed IIa) and partly of a new wave of

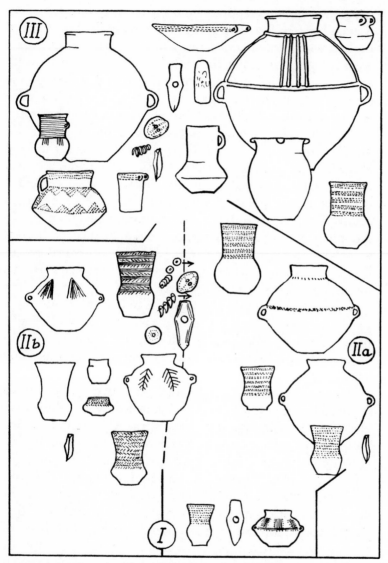

Fig. 16 *Evolutionary chart of Bohemian Corded Ware groups. After M. Buchvaldek*

expansion that now appears from the north (group IIb). The relation between these two groups is not yet quite clear. Corded beakers with everted necks and amphorae with simple orna/ ment are typical of group IIa while beakers with high, expand/ ing necks decorated with herring/bone patterns and amphorae ornamented with fir/twig motifs belong to group IIb. The other pottery varies in a similar way, but we meet in both the groups with the so/called faceted battle/axe. It is probable that this middle phase of the Corded Ware culture comes after the end of the hill/top settlements of the Řivnáč culture which it may have actually destroyed. It is also likely to have coincided with the classic phase of the Bell/Beaker culture discussed below. The last phase (III) is the continuation of group IIa. In this phase we observe the general disappearance of beakers whose place is taken by amphorae, jugs, and pot/shaped vessels. Cord decorations become very rare and battle/axes assume simple, rounded shapes. This phase forms a group which is typical for Bohemia and has analogies only in Moravia. As is proved by grave finds it is contemporary with the undecorated phase of the Bell/Beakers. In Moravia the last phase of the Corded Ware is distinguished by rich graves and some peculiar local shapes.

Plate 35

While the Corded Ware culture originated in the Vistula region, a development from the Channelled Ware culture took place in the wider region of the eastern Alps, leading to the formation of such groups as Vučedol and Ljubljana marsh. Near by and from a similar basis may have originated what is called in Central Europe the Bell/Beaker culture. This cer/ tainly resembles the Vučedol group in both the form and the decoration of its pottery. The shape of its characteristic, flat/ tanged dagger also indicates a region in the neighbourhood of the Eastern Mediterranean, and a connexion with the Alps has recently been confirmed by the spectral analysis of the material of these daggers.

The origin of the Bell-Beaker culture has been much disputed. It is often derived from Spain or even from North Africa but convincing proofs have never been produced. Whatever its native region, the Bell-Beaker culture spread rapidly over Italy as far as Sicily; in the west we meet it in Spain, France, Great Britain, and Ireland; across Central Europe it reached Denmark; and in the east it came to the neighbourhood of Budapest and to the Upper Vistula. This expansion and the contemporary diffusion of the Corded Ware culture complement each other to a great measure, but in Central Europe and especially in Czechoslovakia they overlap. We already know quite a number of finds associating these two cultures but have, so far, no notion about the way in which the people who belonged to them came into contact with each other.

ORIGIN OF THE BELL-BEAKERS

Plenty of remains, especially graves, from the Bell-Beaker culture have been found in Bohemia and Moravia but, up to the present time, none in Slovakia. Although its evolution was not very long, it can provisionally be divided into two phases. Beautifully ornamented reddish beakers and bowls with decorated rims are characteristic of the first phase while in the second phase beakers, as it seems, disappear and only jugs, bowls or pot-like vessels remain. The early stage is probably contemporary with the second phase of the Corded Ware culture, the later stage certainly with its third phase.

Plates 36, 37

Closely related to the Vučedol and Bell-Beaker culture, the Čaka type was diffused over South-West Slovakia. Jug-like shapes and rather small, richly-decorated bowls (of Vučedol ancestry) are characteristic of this group, which is considered as the earlier phase of the Hungarian Nagyrév culture.

ČAKA TYPE

Although of very different origins, the Corded Ware and the Bell-Beaker cultures have a number of features in common and will therefore be treated together.

In Bohemia and Moravia we do not know any settlements of the people with the Corded Ware culture and depend therefore

CORDED WARE BURIALS

on the material from their graves. Today these are flat, though they were originally covered with barrows which have remained preserved only in the forests of North Moravia. The cemeteries for which elevated places were generally chosen, are rather small (five to twelve graves) and the graves do not show any special exterior or interior arrangement with exception of the cover of stones above the grave and one case of a burial in a stone cist. Double burials are rare; usually one person only in a contracted position facing south is interred. Women lie always on the left, men on the right side. In the Moravian barrows the bodies are deposited either in pits, on the level of the soil, or in the cover of the barrow. Traces of the fires that were kept burning during the funerals have been preserved.

BELL-BEAKER
GRAVES

From the Bell-Beaker culture we have settlements as well as graves, but from the former we have not gained any valuable information. In the cemeteries, a ditch round the scalariform burial pit sometimes belongs to the outer arrangement of a grave.

Fig. 17

Other bodies are deposited in stone cists. Traces of wooden constructions, probably funerary chambers, have also been

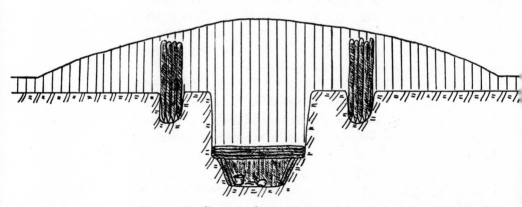

Fig. 17 Smolín, Central Moravia. Section through a reconstructed barrow of the Bell-Beaker culture: around the chamber, built in log-cabin style, is a circular ditch with wooden palisade. Scale 1:100

identified over grave pits. In North Moravia some of the burials under barrows from the culture with Bell-Beakers are in the same cemeteries as the barrows from the Corded Ware culture. Generally the cemeteries of the people using Bell-Beakers are not large though, on an average, they are greater than those of the Corded Ware culture. Inhumation and cremation burials are Plate 38 found in the same cemeteries, and sometimes a cremation burial even appears in the same grave with a flexed skeleton. Cremations are considerably outnumbered by skeleton burials. Uncremated bodies are generally deposited on the right side facing east.

The ornaments used by the people using Corded Ware   ORNAMENTS are characteristic and differ from those of the other Eneolithic tribes in Central Europe. Their love of ornaments is attested by the grave of an old woman discovered at Marefy in Moravia. She had one copper spiral lock-ring on each temple, and wore a necklace of three rows of copper wire coils connected by cross braces. Her clothes were trimmed with a hundred and one bone beads, six thousand one hundred and sixty-four little shell rings, four hundred and twenty-one dog's teeth, and fifty-six bone imitations of such teeth. Dog's teeth were sewn in rows on to the garments of both men and women, and sometimes bracelets or necklaces were made of them. To trim the solemn dress of the woman buried at Marefy, the teeth of more than twenty-two dogs were needed. No wonder that they had to be imitated in bone as there must have been a shortage of real teeth.

Little rings cut from the shells of *Margaritana margaritifera* or *Margaritana auricula* (cardium) served as trinkets for women. Hundreds of these glittering little ornaments covered the dresses, contrasting with the darker colours of the garments. The little discs made from the shells already mentioned were pendant-amulets rather than simple ornaments: they are usually bordered with dots which form also a cross in the middle—

obviously the representation of the solar wheel. In the Corded Ware culture occur also, though seldom, bone pins reminiscent of the hammer-pins from the regions north of the Black Sea. Girdles ended in bone clasps decorated with carvings, and a string connected them.

Ornaments customary with the Corded Ware people, like girdle-clasps, shell rings, and dog's teeth were only exceptionally worn by the Bell-Beaker folk. Their ornaments were of quite another character and in a different taste. Cone-shaped bone buttons, with V-perforations attached in rows, were widely used as trimming to the clothes, although they could also serve to button up the garments. Specimens of amber are very rare but sometimes bone buttons were painted red, obviously to imitate amber. This substance, spreading from the Baltic region over the whole of Central and West Europe, appears already among the people of the Globular Amphorae culture. In exceptional cases bone strips with carved ribs were sewn in rows to the clothes. Bronze pins with hammered and coiled heads were comparatively seldom used. Crescent-shaped pendants made of bone or sometimes also of amber, and decorated with engravings, known from Central Europe, Italy and Sicily, are generally thought to have served as clasps for the fastening of clothes. It is surprising that, so far, they have been reported only from men's graves. Perhaps they were pendants or amulets rather than clasps. With the Bell-Beaker folk necklaces of amber or copper beads also belonged to the personal ornaments category; a necklace of bird's bones is a rarity. Bronze or gold strips fastened to a lining formed some sort of bracelet or diadem, or perhaps were in imitation of wrist-guards.

AGRICULTURE   Not many finds from Czechoslovak territory give evidence of the agriculture of the two cultures of the Late Eneolithic period. But the culture producing Globular Amphorae was an agricultural civilization and it would indeed be astonishing had its off-shoot, the Corded Ware culture, been entirely ignor-ant of agriculture. Evidence of plough cultivation in this culture comes from Denmark, and therefore we must consider agricul-ture as the basis of economy of all the other Central European groups including Czechoslovakia. This assumption cannot be shaken by the circumstance that the graves furnish no proofs of agriculture, since the contents of the graves are dictated by the nature of the rite. With the Bell-Beaker culture the situation is similar, although its vegetable food production is born out by finds of wheat and querns. In both the cultures we have evidence for the breeding of cattle, sheep, goats, and pigs as well as hunting. Dogs must have played a certain part in the economy, and their great number is attested especially for the Corded Ware people.

So far, very few tools are known, as most of the finds come from graves. In the culture with Corded Ware, flat axes of rock with crudely worked surfaces but polished cutting edges appear relatively often but we also find a few small hammer-axes with a saddle for the fastening of hafts; these appear again in a more developed form in the Únětice culture of the Early Bronze Age. In the Bell-Beaker culture small axes of stone as well as of flint are unusually rare. Flaked tools of flint, like knives, end-scrapers, borers, and saws seldom occur in these two cultures. Among bone implements, points, chisels, and awls are worth mentioning while copper tools apart from awls are quite unknown.

SCARCITY OF TOOLS

Stone battle-axes were the typical weapons of the Corded Ware people; the copper battle-axe from Lužice near Hodonín is exceptional. The flat-tanged dagger and the bow and arrow are characteristic of the Bell-Beaker culture, and a mould found at Luděřov in North Moravia was used for the production of copper daggers. These were also imitated in flint, sometimes even through the insertion of blades into the contour of a wooden dagger. An archer's equipment used by the people

WEAPONS

with Bell-Beakers consisted not only of a bow and a quiver with arrows but also of a stone wrist-guard protecting the left wrist against the back-lash of the string. The arrow-heads of flint were made in the shape of a heart or of an elongated triangle with a symmetrically notched base.

DEVELOPMENT OF THE PATRIARCHAL SOCIETY

The conjunction of a low number of settlements, small cemeteries, and the powerful expansion of the cultures of the Late Eneolithic Age is not fortuitous. In the Early and Middle Eneolithic period a considerable improvement (ploughing, increase of stock-breeding, metal-casting, etc.) had been achieved which spread widely in the Late Eneolithic Age. The absence of a settlement architecture indicates that the mobility of the reduced partiarchal societies became greater. Increasing economic prosperity brought about a greater density of population with the result that masses of the inhabitants of Central Europe began to migrate and expanded in all directions.

In the Early and Middle Eneolithic period we have repeatedly noted burials of the leading members of the society; now, in the Corded Ware and Bell-Beaker cultures, this custom was for the first time applied to wider ranks of the prehistoric society, many women and children included. In fact, in the Late Eneolithic Age interments became regular and general.

THE CULT OF THE SUN

The orientation of the burials may point to a cult of the sun. For the Corded Ware culture the nature of this cult is shown by the sparkling shell discs with double-crosses in a circle: symbols of the sun. We have already mentioned the traces of layers of ash in the Moravian barrows indicative of funerary celebrations. There are few other signs of religious rites except various amulets and pendants of bone or amber. The bones of a human hand fastened to the necklace of a member of the Corded Ware culture buried at Praha-Kobylisy certainly make an extraordinary amulet. Within the territory of Czechoslovakia trepanation in prehistory is attested for the people associated with this culture. Opening the skull was probably resorted to in cases of insanity but the motive was ritual rather than curative. A circular ditch at the boundary of a cemetery of the Bell-Beaker folk at Lhánice in Moravia is worth notice: in the delimited area only the traces of two post-holes could be ascertained; it might, therefore, be taken for a primitive form of a circular sanctuary such as are known in West Europe.

The Indo-European problem, which was discussed in the preceding chapter dealing with the Lengyel culture, is usually considered in connexion with the Corded Ware folk. Often the archaeological material has been compressed in order to fit into the conception of the expansion of Indo-Europeans belonging to the Corded Ware culture from the South Russian steppes to Europe. The Corded Ware culture belongs to the family of related Late Eneolithic cultures derived through the Globular Amphorae from the TRB culture, which links it genetically to the preceding Lengyel culture. Attempts to establish a connexion between the Corded Ware culture and all the Indo-European groups have failed one after another. The latest research shows that at the time of the Corded Ware culture the Indo-Europeans must already have been considerably differentiated. On the one hand, the Corded Ware cannot have been a culture of undifferentiated Indo-Europeans; on the other, it must certainly have been an Indo-European culture: but from a study of Bronze Age history it appears that none of the Indo-European nations in Europe have developed out of this group. The Bell-Beaker culture is rarely considered Indo-European but here we have brought it into a possible connexion with the Channelled Ware culture, consequently also with the Funnel-necked Beaker and Lengyel cultures, and we must accordingly consider its bearers as Indo-European. If not the Bell-Beaker culture itself at least the sphere related to it (Čaka-Nagyrév) played a part in the further development of Central Europe and therefore we can consider it as a not fully differentiated

INDO-
EUROPEANS
IN THE LATE
ENEOLITHIC
AGE

Indo-European group from which, in later times, the Central European languages emerged.

The Indo-Europeans who in the Early Neolithic Age came to Central Europe with the Lengyel culture, and developed there in the Early Eneolithic period into the TRB culture, dispersed in the Middle and Late Eneolithic period. The northern groups expanded in the Globular Amphorae and Corded Ware cultures to the east; while the regions of Central Europe remained occupied by the southern branch, developing through the Channelled Ware culture into the Central European group of Indo-Europeans.

CHAPTER IX

The Early Bronze Age

THE Eneolithic Age is usually thought of as ending with the Corded Ware and Bell-Beaker cultures and the Bronze Age as beginning with the following Únětice culture. This division, however, does not correspond to any great economic or social changes but simply marks the appearance of a developed bronze metallurgy, with ornaments far outnumbering axes. The introduction of bronze-working caused no revolution, therefore, and the changes attained in the Eneolithic Age merely took firmer and deeper root.

As already touched on above, the most characteristic and best-known culture of the Early Bronze Age in Czechoslovakia is the Únětice culture. Its territorial extent reached from South-West Slovakia and Lower Austria to Central Germany, Lusatia, and Silesia, whence it penetrated northwards into Greater Poland. In Czechoslovak territory the cultural currents within the limits of this culture came from the south-east, from Moravia and the adjoining parts of Slovakia. North-West Bohemia, often mentioned as the centre of the whole culture, played a more important role only in the late phase when trends towards the formation of a peripheral local group became distinct.

The origin of the Únětice culture is still in some doubt but recent study of the Eneolithic Age has at least resulted in the elimination of some solutions formerly considered possible. From the chronology of the Eneolithic Age it follows that the only cultures that could have taken part in its formation are the

BEGINNINGS
OF THE
BRONZE AGE

THE ÚNĚTICE
CULTURE

87

			SOUTH-WEST BOHEMIA	CENTRAL BOHEMIA	E. BOHEMIA AND N. MORAVIA
Latest Bronze Age	HB			Štítary	Silesian C
		900			
	HA2		V		
			IV		
Late Bronze Age			III		middl
	HA1		II		earl
	BD		Milavče (Vrhaveč) I	Knovíz (Modřany)	Lusatian (Velin
		1300			
	BC		III		
Middle Bronze Age	BB2		Bohemian- Palatinate Middle Danubian Tumuli II	Middle Dan	
	BB1		I		
		1500		V ě t e	
Early Bronze Age	BA2				
	BA1				
		1800			

Chart III Tentative chronol.

OUTH ORAVIA	SOUTH- WEST SLOVAKIA	N./W. AND MIDDLE SLOVAKIA	EAST SLOVAKIA
dolí	Chotín		
	V e l a t i c e	'L u s a t i a n C'	
(lučina)			
			Piliny
ian T u m u l i			
		Eastern Tumuli	
o v	Maďarovce		Otomani
	Hurbanovo		
	Nitra		East Slovak Tumuli
	Mierza- nowice		

he Bronze Age in Czechoslovakia

Corded Ware and the Bell-Beaker culture. The late phases of the Corded Ware culture are well known, and there seems nothing at all to connect it with Únětice culture. On the other hand, there appear very many similarities between the Únětice and the Bell-Beaker culture: in the shapes of vessels (some cups but mainly bowls), in the funerary customs, and in many other details—types of dagger, wrist-guards, stone arrow-heads, etc. It is necessary to bear in mind, however, that many of the Únětice cemeteries occupied the same places as cemeteries of the preceding Bell-Beaker culture. Hence a generic connexion between these two cultures is not impossible. Or it may be that the Únětice culture originated from some south-eastern group of the Nagyrév (Čaka)-Bell-Beaker sphere. In fact, some Moravian finds of Únětician pottery in particular strikingly resemble objects belonging to the Nagyrév culture in Hungary, and the whole character of these two cultures is similar. In this case the so-called Bell-Beaker tradition in the Únětice culture would be explained by the related bases of both the cultures.

In the introductory chapter we noticed the peculiar climatic conditions of the southern part of Bohemia which caused its late occupation by man. Indeed it was not until the Early Bronze Age that prehistoric man began to penetrate it, but when he did so it was from two directions: from the north, Central Bohemia, came the late phases of the Únětice culture, from South Germany came the other current, distinct through its characteristic metallurgy, unknown in Central Bohemia.

The Únětice culture is known from numerous cemeteries as well as from settlements. Its pottery can be classified chronologically. Typical of the earliest phase (I) are pouch-shaped jugs, undecorated or with a poor plastic ornament, and forms reminiscent of the so-called associated pottery of the Bell-Beaker culture (pots with a handle, cups, bowls with a widened rim, and polypod bowls). In this phase graves are almost without bronze grave goods and we do not know of any settlement; this culture has still a Late Eneolithic character. The pottery of the middle phase is distinguished by jug-shaped forms with incised fringes, similar forms of cups, pots, and many types of bowls. The bronze industry (Cypriote knot-headed pins, racquet-, eyelet-, disc-headed pins, lock-rings, etc.) though rare so far, begins to appear in graves as well as segmented faience beads. Only the late, so-called classic phase (III) represents what is commonly thought of as the Únětice culture. Among the funerary pottery the so-called Únětician cups, little spherical vessels, and plain conical bowls are typical. In this period the decoration of ceramic vessels almost disappears again, especially in Bohemia, though persisting farther in the east. The bronze industry, however, undergoes an unprecedented development. Apart from richly decorated daggers and other rarer types we find mostly ornaments in the graves. Various forms of pin serving to fasten the clothes are typical of the Central European Bronze Age: in the Early Bronze Age they are provided with an eye or little ring as a

Plate 40

Fig. 18

Fig. 18   Únětician cup. Krnsko, Central Bohemia. c. 1 : 2

Plate 42

THE
MAD'AROVCE
CULTURE AND
THE VĚTEŘOV
GROUP

precautionary measure against loss. In Únětician graves and hoards we meet many eyelet-, racquet-, disc-, and ring-headed pins. Bracelets of copper bars occur frequently while high cylindrical armlets (cuff-bracelets) are rarer. Coiled basket-shaped lock-rings, sometimes also cast, of bronze or gold wire (*Noppenringe*) are common, while the other types of ornament such as various decorative mountings, platings, larger and smaller bosses appear less frequently. Necklaces consisting mostly of bronze spirals or amber beads were popular. It seems that, at least for Bohemia, it is possible to distinguish a still later phase (IV) of which grave goods like amphora-shaped minia-ture vessels, many necklaces, late types of eyelet pins and some other bronze objects are typical.

At that time the development in Moravia and South-West Slovakia had taken another direction. The Únětice culture gradually developed into the Mad'arovce culture which already belongs to the transition to the Middle Bronze Age. The corresponding development in Moravia is referred to as the Věteřov group. From Bohemia similar finds are known. Interpretation is rendered all the more difficult because the remains come from different spheres: the Únětician material comes almost entirely from cemeteries, the Mad'arovce only from settlements. Therefore we must be careful not to overestimate their apparent differences. From what we know of the Únětice culture we anticipate that the settlement material differs funda-mentally from that of the cemeteries.

Mad'arovce pottery is technically perfect: hard-fired and the surface carefully worked and smoothed. Among the tableware pottery jugs already approaching shapes of the Middle Bronze Age appear again, as well as two-handled amphorae showing the same trend. Barrel-shaped cups on tongue-like legs and plain bowls with a handle are common. The bizarre shape of a cup with chalice-like form developing from the so-called Únětician cup appears comparatively often. Graves being rare

Fig. 19 Typical Věteřov cup. Bánov, S.E.Moravia. c. 1:4

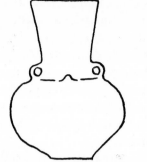

Fig. 20 Amphora and jug of the Maďarovce culture, from Majcichov (left) *and Nitriansky Hrádok* (right) *S.W. Slovakia. c. 1:5*

we do not know the fundamental forms of the bronze in-dustry. Pins with spherical and vertically perforated heads, wire lock-rings, and bar-bracelets with overlapping ends are attested. There are also some bone rings of unknown purpose, sometimes decorated with a complicated geometric pattern which is often compared to a design appearing on certain objects from the Mycenaean sphere, and used for the dating of the Maďarovce culture to some time in the middle of the second millennium: a date also probable for other reasons.

Fig. 21

Brief mention has been made of Slovakian Early Bronze Age cultures, which were in close connexion with the western part of Czechoslovakia. Besides these cultures (Čaka type, Únětice, Maďarovce culture) there existed in Slovakia other Early Bronze Age cultures which came from the northern or southern regions but had no decisive part in the development described above.

Already at the beginning of the Early Bronze Age South-West Slovakia and the adjoining eastern region of Moravia were penetrated from the north by a late branch of the Corded Ware, the Polish Mierzanowice culture. In the graves of this group we find a typical cup whose lower part is decorated with radial cord impressions. Lock-rings in the shape of a willow leaf are typical of the bronze industry.

Fig. 21 Antler ring-let, ornamented with 'Mycenaean' spirals. Věteřov culture. Blučina near Brno. c. 1:3

93

a

b

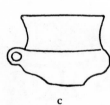

c

THE BRONZE
AGE IN EAST
SLOVAKIA

A certain inheritance from the Mierzanowice culture can be observed in the so-called Nitra type which succeeded it in South-West Slovakia. The essence of this type lies in the material which reveals the closest connexion with the Únětice culture (phase II). Mierzanowice traditions are apparent in its numerous ceramic types (jugs, bowls) as well as in some decorative patterns. Lock-rings in the shape of a willow leaf are of the same ancestry, and faience beads are indicative of cultural connexions.

The Nitra group was followed by a typical culture of the classic Únětician phase. The Danubian part of this culture amalgamated with the southern Kisapostág culture and formed the so-called Hurbanovo type.

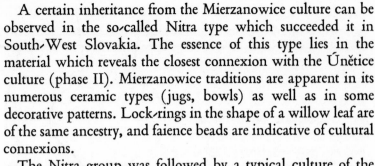

d

Fig. 22 Group of Early Bronze Age pottery, S.W. Slovakia: (a) Mierzanowice cup (Veselé); (b) willow-leaf-shaped lock-ring and (c) vessel, both of the Nitra group (Výčapy-Opatovce); (d) encrusted jug of the Hurbanovo group (Hurbanovo) and (e) profiled cup. c. 1 : 3 (vessels)

In its further development the Únětice culture gave rise to the Mad'arovce culture, while south of the Danube, in Hungary, the culture of the North Pannonian Encrusted Ware develops from the Kisapostág culture. This is why we find many imports of the North Pannonian Encrusted Ware in the Mad'arovce settlements in South-West Slovakia.

In the Early Bronze—as in other periods—East Slovakia was a quite separate region. We meet a late branch of the Corded Ware culture entering this region from the north but this time we cannot say that it belonged to the earliest Bronze Age; much more probably it formed part of the later phase of the Early Bronze Age. This is the culture of the East

Slovakian Tumuli in which we find cremation as well as skeleton burials. Pottery decorated with cord ornament, tumuli, and flint implements point distinctly to the region north of the North-eastern Carpathians.

The next culture that we find in East Slovakia has no traits in common with the preceding one and represents certainly a new expansion from the southern riverine Tisza region in Hungary where, in the meantime, the Otomani (Füzesabony) culture had arisen from the Hatván culture, a continuation of the Nagyrév group. We know from the imports in South-West Slovakia, that the Otomani culture must have flourished at the same times as the Mad'arovce culture even though some of its phases might be a stage older. The ceramic objects of this culture are richly decorated, partly with incisions but mainly with plastic ornamentation set off by channellings. Among the decorated forms jugs with high necks and little bowls are most typical. Naturally, coarse pottery (pots, bowls) prevails in settlements. Besides pottery, birch-bark cups have also remained preserved. The ornaments are made of various materials: we know pins of bronze (disc-headed with plastic decoration) and of bone, showing eastern connexions. Lock-rings of the so-called Transylvanian type of mature shapes appear in bronze and also in gold. Bracelets of bronze bars end in flat spirals. Necklaces consist of amber or faience beads and bronze crescents.

Plate 44

Plate 46

The circumstance that in the Early Bronze Age economy, social structure and spiritual culture appear relatively uniform in all these cultures, allows us to describe them together. But of course, local differences did exist and we will note them in so far as they are known.

Both copper and tin were found in Czechoslovakia in sufficiently large quantities to cover the prehistoric demand. It has been proved by chemical analysis that the first was obtained from the Central Slovakian copper lodes and it is presumed,

THE RAW
MATERIALS
OF BRONZE

95

though without conclusive proof, that the tin came from the deposits in the Bohemian Ore Mountains. For some objects from the Early Bronze Age found in Czechoslovak territory the use of Alpine and Central German ores has been indicated as a result of chemical tests; either is possible and corresponds fully with the cultural currents of that time.

IMPLEMENTS

Most of the preserved bronze objects—ornaments—were of no significance for the economic progress of society. On the whole, the only bronze implement was the axe which, though found in large numbers in some hoards and certainly a common implement, does not seem to have been such a revolutionary invention as is sometimes supposed. It is true that bronze is a better material than stone for the production of axes, but at the beginning of the Bronze Age this quality was counter-balanced by the difficulties in obtaining the required raw materials as well as in working them. In the method of fastening the shafts Early Bronze Age axes are little better than their stone predecessors (one Únětician socketed chisel is an exception). What is more, the method of using bronze axes is almost the same as with stone axes and does not seem to have been more efficient. Nevertheless, bronze axes must have had some advantages over the stone axes as they super-seded them in a comparatively short time. The bronze axes of the Early Bronze Age are flat with widened cutting edges and heightened flanges to grip the cleft part of the shaft.

Fig. 23

Fig. 24

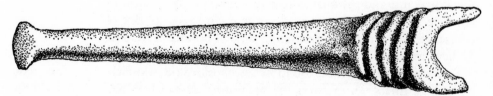

Fig. 23 *Únětician bronze socketed chisel. Vedrovice-Zábrdovice, Central Moravia.* c. 1:3

In addition stone maces also exist resembling one of the types of the preceding Corded Ware culture: the shaft is fastened to a groove ground into the side of the axe. It is a particular type and must have served some special purpose. Flint blades, so far not sufficiently known, were certainly much used as cutting edges for sickles, knives, and arrow-heads because the production in bronze of these important implements had not become established at the time. Finally, bone and antler implements (maces, chisels, awls, needles) still remained in use.

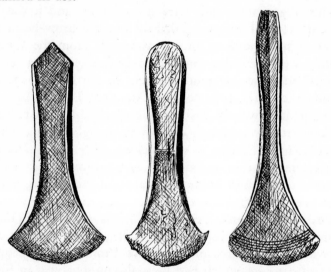

Fig. 24 Bronze axes of the Únětice culture. Left to right: *Soběchleby, Obora (near Nový Bydžov), and Dobřichovice, Bohemia.* c. 2:5

A prominent place among the weapons is taken by triangular bronze daggers which are sometimes richly decorated, the blade with engravings and in some cases the hilt with inlaid bone or amber. Sometimes the hilt is cast in one piece with the blade but more usually it is made of perishable materials and riveted to the blade. Daggers mounted crosswise to the shafts formed

BRONZE
WEAPONS

Fig. 25
Plate 45

97

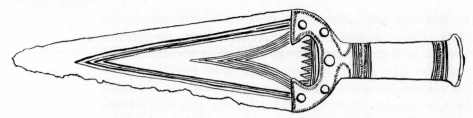

Fig. 25   Únětician bronze dagger, with cast handle. Horoměřice-Kozí Hřbety, near Prague. c. 1:3

halberds but are rare in Czechoslovak territory. In the Early Bronze Age arrow-heads were still of stone, and it was not until the close of this period that the first rare arrow-heads and socketed spear-heads of bronze appeared. From the Únětice culture we know also some stone battle-axes and a few in bronze, the latter are more frequent in the Mad'arovce and Otomani cultures at the decline of the Early Bronze Age.

AGRICULTURE Agriculture was the basis of all Early Bronze Age cultures. It was certainly a plough cultivation though direct evidence from Central Europe is still lacking. All the agricultural implements were of wood or of stone; bronze had not yet penetrated this most important branch of production, and so there were no significant economic and social changes in the course of the Bronze Age. Two kinds of wheat (*Triticum dicoccum* and *T. compactum*), barley, millet, lentils, and peas were grown. The cultures of the Early Bronze Age occupied the fertile regions which had been already inhabited in Eneo-lithic times. The only exception which we cannot yet explain is the new colonization of the less fertile areas of South Bohemia. It indicates either the transition of some tribes to pastoralism or their settlement in regions nearer to the raw materials: the first supposition is the more probable. That the horse had become common is attested by skeletal remains. If at all used as a draught animal then it was most probably to pull the wagons whose existence may be inferred from extant wheel models.

Hunting was still carried on; fishing was improved by the introduction of bronze hooks; and river mussels and turtles were also eaten, as we know from the large numbers of shells from the Únětice, Maďarovce, and Otomani cultures.

We do not know of any settlements from the earliest phases of the Únětice, Mierzanowice, and East Slovakian Tumulus cultures. This is evidently a consequence of the conditions prevailing at that time and during the preceding decline of the Eneolithic Age; of the unsettled way of life and, maybe, of the particular forms of the architecture. But from the Late Únětice culture, Maďarovce culture and its Věteřov type and even from the Otomani culture we know quite a number of settlements. Often they are located on strategic elevations formerly occupied by Eneolithic farmers. These little hill-top settlements are frequently fortified with wooden palisades and ditches, and at Ivanovce near Trenčín (Maďarovce culture), even with a stone wall which, incidentally, appears also in two Věteřov settlements in Moravia. So far there has been no thorough excavation of such settlements of the Únětice culture. We know of houses of the common post construction above ground and of subterranean huts. The houses of the Maďarovce culture have one to three rooms, with the plastering of the inner walls sometimes covered with geometric patterns. At Barca near Košice in East Slovakia a large settlement of the Otomani culture has been systematically excavated. There the rectangular houses stood in regular rows separated by streets two and a half metres wide, the short fronts faced the streets while spaces of about twenty to sixty centimetres separated the adjoining longer side walls of the houses. It was possible to distinguish three types of buildings: one-roomed houses with one fire-place, two-roomed houses with one fire-place and, finally, houses with two rooms each with a fire-place and separated by a third room without a fire-place. The houses may have had wooden floors and furnishings (benches, etc.); the fire-places

Fig. 26

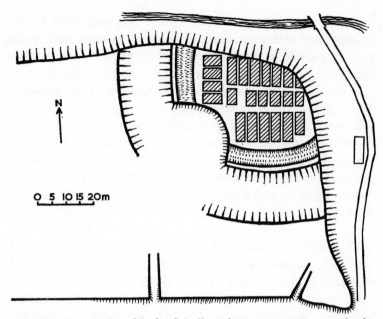

Fig. 26 Schematic plan of the fortified village of Barca, near Košice, E. Slovakia. Otomani culture

or ovens were of clay. Under the debris of the walls were found vessels in a position suggesting that originally they had been on shelves. From the Otomani culture we know also a wood-lined well constructed above a thermal spring which may have had some ritual function.

MEN AT THE HEAD OF SOCIETY

In the era of plough cultivation men's work definitely gained predominance over women's work and this is henceforth reflected in the leading status of men in society. Besides farming and stock-raising, man came increasingly to play a new role, that of the warrior. Fights between tribes are shown to have been very frequent, as much by the abundance of weapons (daggers) as by the doubtless necessary strategic position and fortification of the settlements. Finally also the horse could be used in battle. Knowledge of the arts of war doubtless played a part in the stratification of society, which no longer allowed full equality to all its members. However, the main causes were economic (private ownership of cattle allowing monopoly of the ploughing).

As already stated there were specialists engaged in the work‑ ing of bronze. Considering the small role of bronze imple‑ ments in that period these specialists could not have formed an important group of the population—they were not numerous enough. We must remember that the production of all the objects found in Czechoslovakia datable to the Early Bronze Age would only have occupied one founder for a few years at most. Even admitting that we know perhaps only one‑ thousandth of the actual production, we still do not arrive at a large number of bronze‑founders considering that we have to cover a period of at least three hundred years. Consequently we must presume that the principal subsistence of most of the Early Bronze Age founders lay in agriculture just as with the country blacksmiths of the Middle Ages.

BRONZE SPECIALIZATION

We do not yet know how the raw materials (copper and tin) were acquired and transported. The mining of the raw materials could well have been performed as the seasonal work of the agricultural population in the neighbourhood of the deposits or some groups could periodically have visited the lodes. It does not seem that there existed among the population of the period permanent social groups engaged in mining and living on the proceeds from the exchange of the raw material. But the hoards of ingot‑torcs with terminal loops, even though appearing by the tens and hundreds in the Únětice culture, can be interpreted in favour of either hypothesis.

BARTER

Fig. 27

To suppose itinerant merchants occupying themselves with the exchange of raw material or its products would probably be an anachronism. The trade in bronze was certainly in the hands of the chieftains and extended probably only to the immediate vicinity. The possiblity of long‑distance transport of heavy loads

*Fig. 27   Únětician ingot-torc.
Soběchleby, N.W. Bohemia.* c. 1 : 5

(as well as of their equivalents: corn and cattle) does not seem to fit into the picture of that time. During travels to distant villages, involved in endless fights, any freight of value would certainly have been seized and considered as booty.

GOLD

The trade in bronze was the only one that could have been of economic significance. Of course, there was also a trade in amber which appears frequently in the Late Únětician ceme-teries, and a trade in gold. But it does not seem that in this period gold had become what economists call a 'universal economic equivalent'. It was still relatively rare and used only for the production of little ornaments of the same types as those of bronze, which indicated that, at most, it was considered as a better variant of bronze. In two houses in a settlement of the Otomani culture at Barca near Košice, bronze treasures were found which had probably been kept in open vessels on shelves against the walls. In another contemporary house a hoard of gold had been kept in exactly the same manner which points to similar evaluation of gold and copper.

Plate 43

FAIENCE
BEADS

From the economic standpoint we cannot say much about faience beads, the origin of which, so far without convincing evidence, is usually sought in Egypt. They occur in the Nitra group and in the second phase of the Únětice culture in

Moravia and Bohemia. Consequently they are contemporaneous with the similar beads in Poland and in the Ukraine, but
older than the West European specimens with which they have
probably nothing to do. Moreover the late date attributed to the
first West European specimens is not easily acceptable for
Central Europe. The frequency of their occurrence in the
various regions is interesting for the study of barter in the Early
Bronze Age. Necklaces of faience beads, which have been
found in several graves in the Hungarian cemeteries are a
rarity in the large Moravian cemeteries, and do not occur at all
in Bohemia where single beads appear in only a few graves.
This distribution indicates clearly the gradual advance of faience
beads to the north through inter-tribal barter, but not long-
distance trade carried on by merchants.

PROPERTY

The initial forms of differentiation in property manifesting
themselves in the private ownership of cattle, which we have
noticed in the preceding Eneolithic period, leave no direct traces
in the archaeological remains. But its consequence, the inequality
of the individual members of the patriarchal families, can be
inferred from the many cases in which one member of the
society had to accompany another, probably his superior in life,
into the grave. Otherwise, it seems, the differentiation must still
have been slight. From Únětician and other cemeteries we know
that almost everyone could own a bronze ornament, and in this
period we do not meet with great differences in the grave goods
of the graves. Of course, the hoards of bronze objects tell
another story. Some of them must have represented great wealth
for their time and hardly anyone but the chieftains of prospering
groups could have owned them.

COMPOSITION
OF SOCIETY

Recently it has been ascertained that many Únětician cemeteries do not form a homogenous whole but consist of two to
three little groups of graves comprising twenty graves on an average, of which about thirteen are those of adults. These graves
do not necessarily contain the members of one generation only.

However, as there is no discernible archaeological development in the material (and we are able to distinguish periods to within one hundred years), the number of generations cannot be more than three or four. This corresponds with the fact that one group in these cemeteries comprises two or three double- graves of adults buried at the same time. So regular a custom cannot be interpreted as fortuitous simultaneous death; it is much more probable that some subordinate member of the family was slain on the death of its head, as we find amply proved for Central Europe in the Eneolithic culture with the Globular Amphorae. This would mean two to three genera- tions of chiefs, from which it follows that the grave groups of the Ůnětician cemeteries comprising fifteen to twenty persons covered about two or three generations. Which social units do these groups in the Ůnětician cemeteries represent? At first sight it is clear that they cannot be tribes or clans which, as we know from ethnology, would by far outnumber these groups. But our theory concerning Eneolithic social structure appears to be supported: these units probably represent large patriarchal families, which would correspond perfectly with our numbers.

There arises now the question: which social unit is repre- sented by an entire Ůnětician cemetery? The average number of graves in the known group-cemeteries is about fifty. Other cemeteries which today, for various reasons, cannot be divided into grave groups sometimes exceed this number and reveal a typological development in their material; consequently they belong to many generations. The number of their graves ex- cludes the possibility of considering them as clan cemeteries. Most probably they are cemeteries of the part of a clan living in one homestead. Accordingly we infer that two to three large patriarchal families lived in one community. Up to the present we do not know the size of these settlements but what we know of some fortified hill-top sites, all of which are rather small, would support our hypothesis.

For the Early Bronze Age and the Eneolithic period we have been able to document the social differentiation within the limits of the individual families. The problem of the inner differentiation of the higher social units, the clans, remains open. Únětice culture finds from the so-called princely barrows of Central Germany and Poland indicate that some chieftains attained high social positions. There is nothing to indicate the economic basis of their status, or that it was permanent; probably the chiefs arose through favourable local conditions.

In dependence on social conditions the spiritual culture of the Early Bronze Age did not undergo any great changes. Art had now a decorative character, richer on bronze objects than on ceramics. Decoration consisted simply of geometric patterns. New is the appearance, in the Mad'arovce culture and Věteřov group, of such forms as concentric circles and wave-lines executed with compasses which, together with the spiral, form the complex of decorative elements proceeding from the Mycenaean region and giving a special character to the ornamentation of continental Europe from the Balkans to South Scandinavia in the following Middle Bronze Age.

Sculpture, which was still being produced in the preceding Eneolithic Age, now becomes very rare. In the Únětice culture occur figurines representing cattle and pigs, whose ritual purpose is problematic. In the Otomani culture we frequently find female clay idols with indicated hair styles, necklaces, and parts of garments. We can hardly imagine that their function was the same as that of the Neolithic female idols; they suggest rather a female anthropomorphic deity.

Fig. 28 Barca, near Košice, East Slovakia. Clay figurine with half-moon pendants. Otomani culture. c. 2:3

Apart from the objects just mentioned, evidence of religion comes exclusively from graves. The funerary customs of most of the Early Bronze Age cultures are rather uniform. Contracted inhumation burials are the rule. Only at the decline of the Early Bronze Age can a schism in the conventions of the rite be observed.

Fig. 29

Plate 41

In the Únětice culture we find burials in simple oval pits which are sometimes covered with stones and also in dry-built stone tombs; cists are rare. Some coffins made of hollowed-out tree-trunks have been discovered in favourable soil conditions. For the earliest Únětice culture barrows are known; they disappear later but the graves were certainly provided with surface marks as they do not disturb one another in the cemeteries. The contraction of the skeletons is sometimes so excessive that the arms and legs of the deceased were probably tied together. The majority face east, but a few face south. This orientation points to a cult of the sun which is also indicated by some types of disc-headed pins decorated with concentric ornaments. Both these and some of the clay discs, which are sometimes taken for wagon wheels, probably represent the sun. Cremation burials are very rare, and when they do occur are usually infant burials added to the skeleton burials of adult persons. One particular group among the infant burials, pithos burials known from several Early Bronze Age cultures in

Fig. 29   Únětician   stone-lined grave. Brodce, Central Bohemia. c. *1:30*

Central Europe, indicate influences from the Eastern Mediterranean. Besides graves with one, there exist also graves with two, exceptionally three, deceased persons. At Hlízov near Kolín in an underground hut one man, two women, and four children were buried—obviously a family who perished simultaneously in some catastrophe. The significance of double-graves (man and woman) has already been discussed. In some cemeteries graves with more, consecutive, burials have been found. The skeletal remains of the older burial had been put aside in a heap when the later burial was deposited. There is no doubt that persons thus interred stood in some relation to each other.

In the Mad'arovce culture burials are rare. Up to the present one cemetery in South-West Slovakia with seventy-eight cremation and skeletal burials with different orientations is an exception. In the settlements infant burials in vessels occur; in Moravia we know also of burials of adult persons in domestic pits which contrast with the ritual cremation burials. Probably this contrast is due to social differences but, so far, these two kinds of burial are rare discoveries.

We have but little knowledge of the ritual conventions of the other groups. The Otomani, Mierzanowice, and Nitra groups have contracted skeleton burials, the East Slovakian Tumulus and the North Pannonian Encrusted Ware cultures cremation burials.

From the Únětice culture we know of trepanned skulls and discs removed from skulls in the course of trepanations and worn as amulets. Obviously they represent primitive attempts at a cure for mental diseases, from which it is clear that prehistoric man was already well aware that certain reasoning processes have their seat in the head.

Plate 39

There remains the ethnic problem of the groups whose rich cultures we have described in this chapter. The starting-point of these cultures were two Eneolithic cultural units. The first,

THE ETHNIC
PROBLEM

the culture producing Corded Ware, continued only in the Mierzanowice and East Slovakian Tumulus cultures. Neither of them show any later development and are fully superseded, certainly also ethnically, by cultures originating from the other Late Eneolithic, Nagyrév-Bell-Beaker sphere, to which belong the Únětice, Mad'arovce and Otomani cultures. As set forth in the preceding chapter, both these cultural spheres were Indo-European. But only the one characterized by the Nagyrév and Bell-Beaker cultures gave rise to the next group of Middle and Late Bronze Age cultures from which we can safely derive the Central European branch of Indo-European nations.

CHAPTER X

The Middle, Late, and Latest Bronze Age

THE CULMINATION OF CULTURE DIFFERENTIATION
IN THE PATRIARCHAL SOCIETY FROM
THE FIFTEENTH TO THE EIGHTH CENTURY B.C.

TOWARDS the end of the Early Bronze Age the horizon of the Mad'arovce culture and its Věteřov type spread over most of the former territory of the Únětice culture. In Czecho-slovakia it covered not only South-West Slovakia and Moravia but also East and Central Bohemia, and even appeared in the recently colonized parts of South and South-West Bohemia. Beyond Czechoslovakia it reached as far as Lower Austria, (Böheimkirchen type), South Germany, and probably also Silesia. This horizon genetically connects the Únětice culture with the following complex of the Tumulus culture. It seems that the transition from the Věteřov group to the Tumulus culture took place where the former had occurred in the preceding period. The rise of the Tumulus culture from the Mad'arovce-Věteřov culture can be safely traced in the ceramics and bronze implements as well as in some funerary customs and represents one of the uncontestable facts in Central Euro-pean archaeology.

The Tumulus culture of the Middle Bronze Age forms part of the great complex of related cultures reaching to the eastern boundaries of West Europe and from the Alps to the Baltic Sea, and represents not only the development from the pre-ceding Věteřov horizon but also the consequence of its further expansion to the detriment of the later groups of the Corded Ware culture in the northern parts of Central Europe. Within Czechoslovakia, in consequence of the common basis, its

THE
TUMULUS
CULTURE

earliest horizon is very uniform; differentiation does not take place until later. This gave rise to the Middle Danubian group of the Tumulus culture occupying South-West Slovakia, Moravia, and Central Bohemia while in South-West Bohemia, as in the adjoining part of Germany, the peripheral Bohemian-Palatinate group arose. To this group, whose discovery and subsequent publication is of long standing, greater importance was at first attached than it really deserved. Its expansion into Central and North-West Bohemia was taken for granted but the evidence brought forward in support of this theory proves only that the developments in these regions must have had a common basis, leading naturally to similar results. Of course, the final phase of the Bohemian-Palatinate group differed considerably from the contemporary Middle Danubian group. The peripheral Bohemian-Palatinate group had no further local developments—the Milavče culture in South-West Bohemia is not its continuation but stems from the Central Bohemian group of the Middle Danubian Tumulus culture.

In the Late Bronze Age we find the Velatice culture in South-West Slovakia and South Moravia as well as in the adjacent regions of Hungary and Austria. It sprang from the Middle Danubian group of the Tumulus culture, and the Lausitz culture has not contributed to its creation as used to be thought. The development of the Velatice from the Tumulus culture is one of the certain facts that have been established in the last few years: the perfect continuity of the ceramic and bronze material, in ritual and other spheres of culture, has been recognized.

At the same time the bearers of the Central Bohemian branch of the Middle Danubian Tumulus culture developed their civilization into a new phase termed Knovíz culture. Certain aspects separate the Knovíz from the Velatice culture but hardly any from the Milavče culture in South-West Bohemia. Only the funerary rites differ: in Central Bohemia we meet flat cemeteries while in the Milavče region burials under tumuli are the rule. During later development the differences remained small though a certain differentiation obviously took place. It seems that a further wave of the Knovíz culture, which pre-served its Central Bohemian custom of burying in flat graves, penetrated into the region of Plzeň, the territory of the Milavče culture. The barrows of the Milavče culture are generally interpreted as an inheritance from the older Bohemian-Pala-tinate tumuli inhabitants whose share in the creation of the new culture has not yet been elucidated.

North-East Bohemia and the northern part of Moravia did not participate in the development of the Late Bronze Age that we have been describing. At that time the Lausitz (Lusatian) culture originated in this region from another local branch of the Middle Danubian Tumulus culture. For North-East Bohemia the local development of the Lausitz culture has not yet been demonstrated, and an invasion of the Lausitz culture from adjacent Moravia or Silesia does not seem excluded. Also in Silesia and the adjoining regions the process of the further transformation of the Middle Danubian Tumulus culture into the Lausitz culture took place and caused a very pronounced differentiation within Central Europe: the southern part of the Middle Danubian Tumulus culture continued the tumulus traditions in a way quite different from that of the northern one, which is summarily called the sphere of the Lausitz culture. But, as a rule, within Czechoslovak territory we mean by this term only the culture of the Late Bronze Age: for its continua-tion, from the Latest Bronze Age onwards, other terms are used. Besides the main Lausitz group in North-East Bohemia and North Moravia, we recognize one more Lausitz group which spread in the Elbe region between the northern boundary of the Prague basin and the frontier line of Bohemia in the north. This is clearly connected with similar material found in East Germany and forms part of their further development. So

THE LAUSITZ
CULTURE

far, its domestic roots have not been ascertained and, probably, it represents a southward expansion from East Germany along the river Elbe. As we shall see later, it was the only Lausitz expansion towards the south into the former tumuli territory and led not to the creation of a mixed group but to a stable local branch.

In the westernmost projection of Bohemia (district of Cheb) and on the Upper Ohře it is possible to recognize another group which is sometimes called Lausitz. But these finds are connected directly neither with the Lausitz culture nor with the Knovíz culture of Central Bohemia.

NO LAUSITZ
EXPANSION

The Lausitz culture was often used to provide far-reaching theories explaining the origin of the Velatice, Knovíz, South German Urnfield and sometimes even more remote cultures by postulating its vigorous expansion southward. Recent investigations have demonstrated that all of these cultures had their native roots in the Tumulus culture. Moreover, they proved to be as old as, or even older than, the earliest undisputable manifestation of the Lausitz culture. It was revealed that no finds representing the Lausitz culture during its expansion existed south of the Lausitz territory in North-East Bohemia and North Moravia.

The boundaries between the Lausitz culture on the one hand, and the Knovíz and Velatice cultures on the other, did not remain quite stationary. In the course of the later development minor displacements of the Lausitz culture to the south, and vice versa, took place. These shifts occurred rather late and covered only some tens of kilometres so that they could not have exerted any influence on the origin of the above-mentioned southern cultures.

Thus the once firmly-established theory of the expansion and great importance to Central Europe of the Lausitz culture turned out to be unfounded: on the contrary, it was the south which influenced the Lausitz culture.

Through direct development the Podolí culture derives from the Velatice in South Moravia, South-West Slovakia (here called the Chotín type), and the adjoining regions: while in Bohemia the Knovíz culture continues in the Štítary type. Recent research has shown that similar changes also occurred in the sphere of the Milavče culture, where the continuity with the succeeding period has been established. The divergence of the developments in Bohemia on the one hand, and in the Moravo-Slovakian regions on the other, resulted during this latest period in the formation of two distinctly different groups: the Podolí culture and the Štítary type. The deviations from the northern groups of the former Lausitz culture (represented in this late phase by the Silesian culture) persist or increase. The origin of the Silesian in the Lausitz culture appears proved for North Moravia but is often contested for North-East Bohemia: in that case the Silesian culture in North-East Bohemia would be the result of an expansion from Moravia or adjacent Silesia, i.e. an ethnic dislocation very rare in the Late Bronze Age.

OTHER GROUPS OF THE LATEST BRONZE AGE

At the beginning of the Middle Bronze Age we find in Central Slovakia the so-called Eastern Tumulus culture. Although comprising distinct Otomani features, the origin of this culture usually gets connected with the Mad'arovce culture. The rest of the period is taken up by cultures which developed from Early Bronze Age elements. They are known under the comprehensive denomination, Piliny culture, which spread in East and Central Slovakia and in the adjacent territories of Hungary (Zagyvapálfálva) and lasted during the whole of the Middle and Late Bronze Age.

SLOVAKIA

We have briefly described the very intricate development from the Middle to the Latest Bronze Age in Czechoslovakia. Before we proceed to a critical examination of the general character of the whole period we shall try to give a concise description of some of the archaeological features of the various culture groups.

We know the remains of the Middle Danubian Tumulus culture from both cemeteries and settlements, those of the Bohemian-Palatinate group from cemeteries only. So far, our knowledge of the settlements of the Middle Danubian Tumulus culture is rather slight: sometimes they are located in strategic positions. The cemeteries of both the groups are bi-ritual under barrows. The barrows are of circular or elliptical plan and often they cover an interior stone construction and several burials. The number of barrows in one cemetery generally does not exceed fifty. Most barrows occur in South Bohemia where they have remained preserved in the forests; in populated and cultivated regions they were destroyed long before any interest in archaeology existed.

Plate 48

It is mainly pottery that is found in settlements and graves. It comprises amphorae, various types of bowls (some of them pedestalled), pots, jugs with high necks and ribbon handles, and also various types of coarse ware. The decoration of the ceramic objects of the Middle Danubian group consists mostly of relief (wall-shaping through inside pressure, channelling), but pottery with incisions similar to those of the Bohemian-

Fig. 30

Palatinate group of which the ladder motif is particularly typical also existed. Hoards of clay vessels evidently directly connected with potters' workshops have been reported.

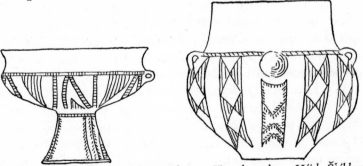

Fig. 30   Pottery of the Bohemian-Palatinate Tumulus culture. Hájek-Šťáhlavy near Plzeň. c. 1 : 4

In comparison with the preceding period, the bronze material of the Tumulus culture had increased considerably. Among the ornaments there appear many types of pin, of which the earlier ones have bulb-shaped, vertically perforated or bi-conical heads with a diversely-shaped shank and a strength-ened, perforated neck. The later ones have plain heads and pins but their necks are richly decorated with plastic orna-ments or incisions. Tutuli sown to the garments enjoyed great popularity. Bracelets of various shapes (spiral, rod, and sheet bracelets) are usually covered with an elaborate, engraved decoration. Necklaces comprise amber beads, beads of a vitre-ous substance, bronze spirals, heart- and disc-shaped bronze pendants, while recoiled lock-rings appear also in gold. Articles connected with the toilet appear for the first time to form a new category of bronze objects: tweezers and double-edged, round-shaped razors with ring handles at their ends. Among the other bronze implements, too, new types turn up. Awls and

Fig. 31 Bracelets of the Middle Danubian Tumulus culture from Central Bohemia. Krupá (above) and Nymburk (below). c. 2:5

Fig. 32

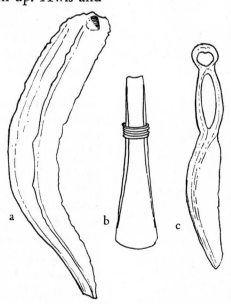

Fig. 32 Working tools of the Middle Danubian Tumulus culture from Central Bohemia: (a) sickle, (b) axe with wire for fastening, (c) knife, Minice, Malnice, Stará Boleslav. c. 2:3, 1:3, 1:2

a   b   c

Fig. 33

Plate 47

axes of various shapes (flanged, with a stop-ridge, or winged) were joined by bronze sickles and knives with cast hilts always ending in rings. A fragment of a bronze saw has also been reported. The weapons, too, appear in many more shapes. Already in the early phase of the Tumulus culture the length of riveted daggers increased considerably, and in the late phase we meet with real swords having massive, cast hilts of oval or octagonal cross-section and ending in a disc-pommel. Some of the swords had hilts of perishable materials riveted to their tangs. Bronze spear-heads, arrow-heads and flat battle-axes with shaft tubes parallel to their edges and disc- or fan-shaped butt-ends were common: they prevailed in the early phase of the Tumulus culture. The raw materials for the production of bronze were no longer transported in the form of ingot-torcs but of rib-shaped bars.

Fig. 33   Tachlovice, Central Bohemia. Sword with richly decorated cast handle. Middle Danubian Tumulus culture. c. 1 : 2

Fig. 34

In the sphere of religion we meet for the first time with distinctively recognizable offering-places. The remains of little clay altars with plastic and painted decorations, and other objects (clay models, burnt wheat, remains of sacrificed animals, etc.) reveal a mature form of ritual.

THE PILINY
CULTURE

Up to the present the Piliny culture has been mainly known from cremation graves which sometimes form large urnfields. The pottery, showing distinctly the traditions of the Otomani and Eastern Tumulus cultures, is mainly represented by great amphora-shaped vessels, jugs, and bowls. Their surfaces are well smoothed, the proportions of the forms are balanced, with channelled or incised decoration.

Fig. 34 Cult-object (? altar) of clay daub with applied decoration. Middle Danubian Tumulus culture. Černý Vůl, near Prague. c. 1 : 2

The bronze industry of the Piliny culture is similar to that of the Tumulus culture. The inventory is enlarged by the earliest socketed axes and some other types that do not occur in the west. A lead ring is a novelty. Besides ornaments, bronze tweezers and lunula-shaped razors are also found. From among the implements various types of axes and sickles deserve special notice, and among the weapons, swords with cast octagonal hilts or tangs, daggers, battle-axes, spear- and arrow-heads. The isolated position of some of these hoards in the mountains on either side of the Carpathians gives evidence of the lively trade from the Carpathian basin to the north.

Plate 51

The Velatice culture is also predominantly known from cremation graves combining to form whole urnfields. In this period barrows disappear but the grave pits are sometimes lined with stones. At Blučina near Brno a settlement fortified with a ditch about eight hundred metres long and a stone rampart has been excavated. In the ditch, among and under the stones of the collapsed wall were about two hundred human skeletons.

THE VELATICE
CULTURE

117

Plate 53

They include ritual burials with grave goods as well as ran-domly positioned skeletons, single skulls, or heaps of bones. It is obviously the consequence of a raid on the settlement and the subsequent massacre of the inhabitants: hence the mutilated bodies and the careless skeleton burials—normally cremation burials were the rule in the Velatice culture.

Plates 54, 55

The pottery vessels of the Velatice culture are technically superb, richly shaped but seldom decorated. They comprise amphorae, bi-conical vessels, storage jars, and numerous bowl-shaped cups whose handles reach far above their rims. Coarse ware is usually decorated by means of 'fingering': finger-tip grooves roughening the surface of the vessel. Rims turned out horizontally are characteristic of amphorae. The earliest shapes derive directly from Tumulus forms and are therefore more reminiscent of the North Moravian Lausitz culture than the later shapes which were already beginning to arise from the diverging development.

We know the bronze objects of the Velatice culture from graves and from hoards. From the latter come not only finished products but also loaf-shaped lumps of raw bronze and broken objects which had been collected to be re-cast. Some bronze axes have wings for the fastening of the shafts, others are socketed. Among the implements, chisels, knives, and sickles also appear; among the weapons, swords with cast hilts of the so-called Liptov type, and, sporadically, daggers, and bronze spear- and arrow-heads. Long pins with richly shaped heads persist among the ornaments. Bracelets are made of metal rods or are flat and ribbed, terminating in spirals. Fibulae with decorative plaques are probably of northern origin. Razors are round as in the Tumulus and Knovíz cultures. Bronze vessels, especially cups which probably originated within the sphere of the Velatice culture from native ceramic patterns, widen the material's range.

Among the ritual objects we find again a little zoomorphic vessel in the shape of a bull with a funnel on top and an outlet at the back. Little bronze wheels with four spokes are usually taken for symbols of the sun: probably correctly, as the cult of the sun was universally practised in the Bronze Age.

The Podolí culture originated through native development from the Velatice and occupied the same territory. Its graves contain cremation burials and are sometimes surrounded with a circle of stones so that it seems fairly likely that originally they were covered with barrows. The settlements occupy elevations sometimes fortified with powerful ramparts. Among the pottery vessels amphorae predominate, approaching flasks in shape, and plain bowls with inverted rims. Channellings with incised, star-like ornaments often decorate the pottery inside. The razors of the Podolí culture are lunate and therefore probably of southern origin. From the other bronze objects a model of a horse from Obřany near Brno deserves notice. For this period the first use of iron objects has been attested.

THE PODOLÍ CULTURE

Plates 57, 58

The Knovíz culture arose in Central and North-West Bohemia in the same manner as the Velatice culture in South Moravia and South-West Slovakia. Sometimes the settlements were surrounded with a ditch and the plastering of the walls inside the dwellings was painted with white and red geometric patterns. Bell-shaped pits which are common in the Knovíz settlements probably served for the storing of cereals. The cemeteries are small and contained cremation burials in flat graves. We know also of inhumation burials in domestic pits, sometimes placed in a ritual position, sometimes not and without grave goods: the varying form of the rite obviously reflects social differences. The bones found in the settlement pits are sometimes intentionally cast away or even mutilated, and this, together with the fact that split and burned human bones have been found among refuse and animal bones, may be due to cannibalism—evidently motivated by the rite.

THE KNOVÍZ CULTURE

In graves and cemeteries the ceramic objects are usually of a good technical standard. Large storage vessels up to a metre in

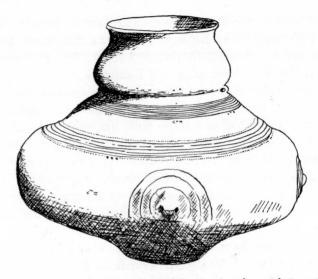

Fig. 35   Storeyed urn (Etagengefäss) *of the Knovíz culture. Plaňany, Central Bohemia.* c. 1:4

height have also been found, evidently used for storage of small quantities of corn. Their surfaces, as well of those of smaller pots with two handles at their rims, are roughened by means of finger-tip ornamentation in contradistinction to the carefully finished amphorae, and the bi-conical vessels and cups, which are often covered with a graphite slip to give them lustrous surfaces. Most often the decoration is channelled, rarely incised. The pottery of the Knovíz culture had a very long development which can be divided into five phases according to the alterations in profile.

The bronze industry in the Knovíz culture continued the traditions of the Tumulus culture. Among the ornaments found are pins with elaborate heads and large shield fibulae ending in spiral discs. Bracelets are made of bronze sheet or spirals of bronze, and the larger ones of bronze rods. We find also torcs, necklaces of amber or glass beads, rings, various

Fig. 35

THE KNOVÍZ
BRONZE
INDUSTRY

Plate 49

button-like ornaments for garments and girdle-clasps. Among the implements of the Knovíz culture flat-winged as well as socketed axes occur. Bronze sickles, tanged knives and circular razors with ring-ended handles are numerous. Swords with cast hilts (the so-called Liptov type) occur with the so-called Auvernier swords whose pommels are saddle-shaped. Spear- and arrow-heads belong to the equipment too. As in the Velatice so also in the Knovíz culture we find several types of bronze vessels. Here, too, it seems that the later ones imitate clay forms from the repertoire of the Knovíz pottery.

Fig. 36

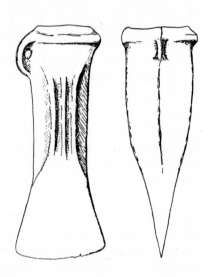

Fig. 36 Socketed bronze axe from the Maškovice hoard, N.W. Bohemia. c. 1 : 2

In the Latest Bronze Age the Štítary type is the continuation of the Knovíz culture. It is worth remarking that in the domestic pottery the finger-tip roughening of the surface is superseded by vertical grooves executed with a comb. Also the bi-conical vessels disappear and the other ceramic objects acquire angular shapes. The Štítary type probably did not have as long a duration as the preceding phases of the Knovíz culture.

THE ŠTÍTARY TYPE

THE MILAVČE
CULTURE

The differences between the Knovíz and the Milavče cultures are very small. The Milavče culture is mainly known from cemeteries in which the burials are not in flat graves but under barrows. Cemeteries with flat graves form a particular group in the region of Plzeň which shows close connexions with Central Bohemia, though some types of knife from the graves of the Milavče culture find analogies rather in neighbouring Germany than in Central Bohemia, in the region of the Knovíz culture. Other exceptional finds include a small bronze cauldron on a four-wheeled cast undercarriage from Milavče near Domažlice: it has the form of a large bronze cup and is evidently a native product. The settlements of the Milavče culture are little known but the existence of fortifications in strategic positions is attested. Some of them are extensive (areas of up to fifty hectares have been reported) and surrounded by a tumble of earthwork, the remains of a timber-laced stone and clay rampart.

THE LAUSITZ
URNFIELDS

In its initial stages the Lausitz culture which occupied the northern part of the territory of Czechoslovakia differed little from the adjoining southern cultures (Velatice, Knovíz), although greater differences arose during its later development. We know of it partly from ruined settlements but mainly from cemeteries. Some of the settlements occupied elevated positions and were fortified with ramparts and ditches. The dwellings, measuring approximately ten by seven metres, were blockhouse constructions and had two rooms. The graves form the well-known urnfields, some of which are very extensive and were used over long periods. Cremation was universally practised; the collected bones were brought to the graves from the special cremation places. Not all the bones were gathered but they always included a part of the head and thorax; they were deposited in simple pits (pit graves) or in one of the double jars used as a funerary urn (urn graves). Of course, many other combinations in the way of depositing earthly remains are known. In the Lausitz culture graves under barrows occur; at another time they retain at least the stone constructions known from the tumuli. However as might be expected flat graves are the rule.

Pottery objects appear in large numbers but their manu-facture differs according to whether they come from graves or from settlements. The funerary pottery is often less carefully fired and crumbles easily. In the graves amphorae and bi-conical vessels, various types of bowls, cups, and coarse pots with two handles under the rim are most frequent. In the early phase, breast-like protuberances at the widest parts of amphorae and jugs are often met with. Incised lines border these projec-tions in East Bohemia and North Moravia, while plastic grooves mark them off in the group on the Lower Elbe. These two Lausitz groups also differ considerably in other details of the pottery. In the late phase of the Lausitz culture, Velatice and Knovíz influences are evident in the application of graphite and channelling.

THE LAUSITZ
GROUPS

Fig. 37

Plate 56

Fig. 37   Lausitz pottery: (a) amphora and (b) bi-conical vessel, Jaroměř, N.E. Bohemia. c. 1:3

The bronze industry is very varied. Among the ornaments we find lock-rings, rings, bracelets, torcs, necklaces of little bronze tubes and glass beads. Pins have various heads. In the Lausitz culture we meet more often with large fibulae consisting of two parts and provided with decorative shields and spirals. In gold it yielded an ornament of wire coiled twice in the shape of the figure 8—probably a form of keeping precious raw materials as it could hardly have served any practical purpose because of its weight. Also the gold axe from Sokoleč near Poděbrady weighing three-quarters of a kilogram could not have had a practical function: it too was either a form of storing raw material or a cult-object, perhaps a social insignia.

The bronze implements include winged axes, knives, awls, and sickles. The razors are chopper-shaped, single-edged, and decorated with engravings—the southern type of circular razor is less often found. We know comparatively little of weapons as they were not usually deposited in the graves and few hoards have been discovered. Spears, stone and bone arrow-heads, swords of the Liptov type as well as tanged swords with hilts of organic materials occur.

Cult-objects found in the graves include little zoomorphic vessels, mostly representing bulls, bronze wheels, perhaps symbols of the sun, and axes of soft minerals that may have had a ritual significance.

THE SILESIAN URNFIELD CULTURE

The Silesian culture which succeeded the Lausitz in its inhabitation area resembled it very closely. Among its funerary rites cremation burials of several individuals in one grave have been attested; the question arises whether they are to be interpreted as the simultaneous burial of several persons or otherwise.

The bronze industry comprised smaller types of pin with vase-like heads, pendants and torcs and the last specimens of the large fibulae with embossed or engraved plaques. Among the implements socketed axes outnumber the older winged type.

Plate 50

Plate 52

Plate 61

The cult of the sun is attested by the fittings in the form of aquatic birds from Svijany near Turnov in North-East Bohemia —perhaps parts of a little cult-wagon as we know them from neighbouring Lausitz. Here moon-shaped idols (*Mondidole*), clay moon-sculptures on clay discs appear for the first time, just as in the contemporary Štítary type of the Knovíz culture. Of course, their connexion with the cult of the moon is hypo-thetical. Clay rattles are found in the graves of adults as well as of children: therefore they were probably cult-objects rather than toys.

There is no evidence to indicate that the Early, Middle, Late, or Latest Bronze Age brought about revolutionary changes in the economy or society. ECONOMIC CHANGES

Stone was now almost entirely superseded in the manu-facture of implements, but bone and antler were still used for such things as chisels, awls, and maces. Bronze axes underwent a long development from the forms with a stop-ridge to the winged shapes: this evolution can be seen in Czechoslovak territory also. But already, from the Middle Bronze Age on-wards, socketed axes which had developed in the east began to appear. Although their production was more economic than that of flat axes (less bronze was needed for the same length of edge) they did not supplant the native types until the Latest Bronze Age.

In the Middle Bronze Age we find among the tools new types of knife and also bronze sickles which are the only agricultural implement made of bronze—the others, especially the plough, were still of wood. At that time the knowledge of bronze affected agriculture only little—though it is true that the manufacture of wooden implements was made easier than it had been before by the use of bronze knives and axes. But that was only a trifling part of the required work and was of no revolutionary significance for society. Agriculture remained the principal source of subsistence, as evidenced by AGRICULTURE the many finds of vegetable remains from the cultures that we have discussed. Cattle-breeding played an important part and it seems that it actually predominated in some less fertile regions (for example, the southern parts of Bohemia) and became there the specialization of the local inhabitants of the Tumulus and Milavče cultures.

BARTER
Plate 59

There is no proof of a substantial increase in barter. Trade was still mainly confined to ornaments and comparable objects. The composition of some of the hoards indicates that they consisted of personal property: for example, a dagger, a spear, and an axe held together by a bracelet were found at Blučina near Brno (Velatice culture). We do not know the reason for the deposition of the hoards which, consequently, do not give any evidence concerning the development of exchange. The hoards of bronze swords in North Slovakia are perhaps an exception. There some hoards containing several specimens (up to six) have been found while in graves only single swords occur. This is accounted for by the fact that from there, the region of their production, they were bartered to the whole of Central Europe.

PROPERTY

So far, there is little evidence concerning property. Land was not yet in private hands but ownership of cattle and consequently also use of the plough drawn by it doubtless remained the privilege of certain individuals. On the other hand, small amounts of property, especially of bronze objects, remained within the range of everyone as we know from graves. This applies to all ornaments with the exception of ostentatious bronze fibulae. Some of the specifically masculine material could hardly have been owned by anyone but the chieftain of a large group. Into this category fall the bronze swords that we have mentioned, and the sets of drinking-vessels (bronze buckets, cups, or strainers in various combinations). Generally they are found in graves of outstanding richness, and are often associated with swords. It is not impossible that these vessels were being used already in the Late Bronze Age, as later in Roman times, for the drinking of wine which is known to have been imported into Central Europe during the following later phase of the Hallstatt period.

Exceptionally equipped graves with swords, ornaments, and sets of vessels do not appear until the Velatice and Knovíz cultures. We can follow the steady development of war-fare, which is clear not only from the quantity of weapons and their continuous improvement but also from the increasing stress laid upon the strategic position and fortification of the settlements. The skeletons found in the defence ditch at Blučina which we have mentioned above are an eloquent testimony to the conditions of the time. Exceptionally equipped graves always belong to men and prove that the patriarchal organiza-tion was gaining in strength but had not reached the point at which the heads of the families formed a special social class: such a class nearly always manifests itself by raising whole families to prominence, and is documented archaeologically by conspicuous burials of women and children, too.

In religion we can prove the continuation of the Sun cult and the great development of ritual which found expression in special places reserved for the cult. Unfortunately we know the details only of the funerary rites. In the cultures of the Middle Bronze Age the burials were still bi-ritual but gradually crema-tion began to prevail and became almost the only rite in the Late and Latest Bronze Age. Even leaving the extraordinary character of the Velatician burials at Blučina out of account, there still remain in the settlements of the Late Bronze Age, many inhumations, and the position of some of these burials is not ritual. As there is no reason to suppose a Lausitz expansion, we can hardly say that this anomaly corresponds to an ethnic difference between the people buried in cremation graves on the one hand, and those buried in the settlements on the other. It probably reflects the following progressive social differentiation:

obviously poor or non-ritual burials belong to individuals who ranked lowest in the society of that time and were not entitled to a posthumous life secured to the others through ritual cremation burials. Strange finds from the region of the Piliny culture of the Latest Bronze Age are masks cut from human skulls: probably they served ritual purposes though we are not yet able to define their functions.

INDO-
EUROPEANS

There remains the problem of the ethnic provenance of the cultures of the Middle, Late, and Latest Bronze Age. In these periods we get considerably closer to the epoch in which at least some Indo-European nations of the Central European group begin to appear in written records. All the civilizations dealt with in this chapter can be derived from the Únětice through the Tumulus and Věteřov-Mad'arovce cultures, and belong to the typically Central European sequence traceable from the Late Neolithic Age: they are certainly Indo-European groups.

The divergence of the Tumulus sphere into the northern Lausitz and the southern Velatice-Knovíz cultures was obviously of momentous importance to subsequent ethnic group-ings. From the Knovíz culture onwards a continuous develop-ment to those groups which (on the basis of later written records) must be considered Celtic can be traced, and the Velatice culture is probably a similar case. From the Lausitz culture and others related to it to the north of Czechoslovakia, came groups which subsequently developed into the cul-tures of the German, Baltic, and Slavonic nations. But the Lausitz culture in Czechoslovakia can hardly be included in one of these national groups as it lies too far outside the sup-posed area of their formation. We must remember, moreover, that in Central Europe, after the long development from the Middle to the Latest Bronze Age, other Indo-European language groups could also have formed, whose names are not found in the later written records since by then they were of no consequence or no longer existed.

CHAPTER XI

The Early Iron Age and Early La Tène Period

THE RULE OF THE WARRIOR CASTE
FROM THE SEVENTH TO THE FOURTH CENTURY B.C.

AFTER the extreme variations of the Latest Bronze Age we observe in the Hallstatt and Early La Tène periods the beginning of a levelling of the various cultures. The individual culture groups of the preceding period, continuing their development, acquired many common features which brought them nearer to one another. From the point of view of archaeology this process manifests itself most strikingly in the pottery. In the settlements of this period prehistoric pottery, after the great multiplicity of shapes in the Late and Latest Bronze Age, gradually gives way to a pottery little differentiated in shape and, though technically perfect, of simple functional forms—pots and bowls. In the graves the richness of shapes continues at least in the beginning of this period but the vessels are less characteristic of their respective countries. The same trend is seen again in the decoration, painted or delicately incised, reflecting the so-called Hallstatt style which is characterized by perfectly balanced, geometric decorations.

THE LEVELLING OF CULTURES

Bronze types were spreading far outside the natural boundaries of the little culture groups already in earlier periods and the newly introduced iron articles equalled, perhaps surpassed, them in this respect. Both were levelling factors obliterating local cultural distinctions; nearly all metal ornaments are decorated or shaped in Hallstatt style. Relatively great variability still persisted, however, in the funerary rite; many graves, particularly the rich ones, have a really individual character.

The development in the region of the former Podolí culture in Moravia and of the Chotín type in South-West Slovakia

SEREĎ TYPE

continued into the Hallstatt period. In the territory of the Chotín type of the Podolí culture we now find the Sereď type of the Kalenderberg culture, which spread also into the adjoining parts of Austria. This type has cremation burials in pit graves without barrows; inhumation burials are rare. The funerary pottery displays a great variety of forms and is generally decor-ated with incised geometric patterns, seldom with red paintings.

THE HORÁKOV
CULTURE

The related Horákov culture developed in South Moravia from the Podolí culture. Evidence of its material culture comes from the settlements which are often fortified and also from tumulus cemeteries. They comprise cremation or skeleton burials

Plate 63

or even both these rites, and the great barrows—up to five metres high—cover underground log-chambers. Under the smaller barrows the burials are usually deposited on the level of the surrounding ground surface but cremation burials without barrows are not unknown. The burial in the cave of Býčí skála in Moravia also belongs to the Horákov culture; this will be

Fig. 38

discussed later. In the graves are large, funnel-necked storage vessels, amphorae, bowls, and cups in great numbers. The geometric decoration is incised, seldom painted. The bronze bowl with embossed aquatic birds is thought to be an import

Fig. 38 Bulbous vessel of the Horákov culture. Horní Dunajovice, S.W. Mora-via. c. 1:5

from the south. Among the ornaments we still meet with the figure-of-eight brooch of wound bronze wire but also the boat and harp brooches which both here and elsewhere became typical of this period. Necklaces of amber beads, bracelets, and finger-rings are common; the late forms of bronze pins are also still being produced.

The Bylany culture in Central and North-West Bohemia resembles the Horákov culture in many aspects. It developed locally from the Štítary type of the Latest Bronze Age. So far, we know of very few settlements, and from these scarcely anything other than pottery. Barrel-shaped pots with smoothed necks and bowls with inverted rims prevail. But from the flat crema-tion graves come many types of vessel: large funnel-necked storage vessels, bowls, plates, and various types of cup. Graphite coating, incisions and red, brown, or black paintings often decorate the pottery. The applied decorations are in the geo-metric Hallstatt style. Besides pottery, embossed metal cups appear.

THE BYLANY
CULTURE

Plate 62

In the large, so-called princely barrows of the Bylany culture, sometimes comprising skeleton burials, the remains of wagons have been found with numerous items of their furniture. The wagon from Hradenín near Kolín was four-wheeled, its gauge about one hundred and ten centimetres. The wheels have a diameter of eighty centimetres, and are provided with iron tyres on wooden felloes from which spokes run to the iron hub fixed at the axle-tree. By means of the draught-pole, horses, traces of which are lacking in the graves, were put to the wagon; the bits are made of iron, while the wooden yokes are covered with leather and studded with bronze tacks in geo-metric patterns. Similar tacks and various mountings decorate the rest of the harness so that the whole turn-out must have presented a magnificent appearance.

In the graves many ornaments were found. The swan's-neck pins are small. Among the brooches appear double spiral, harp,

and drum types; among the bracelets, the earliest made of sapro-
pelite as well as simple armlets of metal rods with expanded
terminals. Necklaces of yellow glass beads with blue-white
dots are typical of that time.

As the Latest Bronze Age in South and South-West
Bohemia has not yet been sufficiently elucidated we are not able
to furnish evidence for the continuity of the development from
the Milavče to the Tumulus culture of the Hallstatt period. Such
a continuity seems very probable because the universal trend
paralleled that of Central Bohemia. The Tumulus culture is
also known from settlements, many of which occupy defensible
positions and are fortified. Cremation is the only funerary rite.
The burials are usually on the level of the surrounding ground
surface and covered with small barrows. In the region of Plzeň
some barrows cover chambered tombs resembling those of the
Central Bohemian Bylany culture: in their quadrangular pits
appear up to sixty vessels. Horse-gear and parts of wagons
occur too. The shapes and decorations of the pottery approach
those of the Bylany culture but painted vessels are found less
often than in Central Bohemia. Grave vessels are typically
funerary: the contemporary domestic pottery shows fewer
shapes but is technically better made.

The hollow rings of bronze sheet covered with delicately
engraved decorations are typical of the Tumulus culture. They
were probably worn as bracelets and anklets. Among the
brooches some take the form of a figure-of-eight, others are
serpent-shaped; there are even Certosa brooches. Wire neck-
rings ending in hooks, necklaces of amber and yellow glass
beads with blue dots, or of blue beads with white zigzag lines
adorned the neck.

Sometimes we find bronze vessels: buckets of corrugated
bronze sheet or cauldrons provided with cross-shaped attach-
ments for the handle.

The Platěnice culture arose gradually from the Silesian

culture, and is still substantially different from the Kalenderberg, Horákov, Bylany, and Tumulus cultures. We know it
almost exclusively from its urnfield cemeteries. The votive
vessels are usually arranged in rows in oval pits. Double-burials
are rare.

THE
PLATĚNICE
CULTURE

The Platěnice pottery represents a further stage of the Silesian
culture, and comprises amphora-shaped vessels with protuberances on their bases, situla-shaped cups, coarse pots, cups,
bowls, plates, and strainers. The decoration usually takes the
form of applied graphite or incisions.

Fig. 39

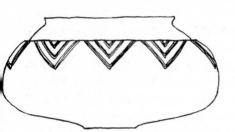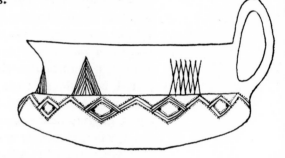

Fig. 39   Vessels of the Platěnice culture. Jaroměř, N.E. Bohemia. 1 : 4

Whole wagons have not been found in the graves, but a
four-wheeled wagon drawn by a pair of horses appears engraved on the handle of a knife from Dobrčice in North
Moravia, and in other graves parts of harnesses and wagon-
fittings have been found. Ornaments are not very numerous.
Pins are small and often of the swan's-neck variety, brooches are
of iron or of bronze. Harp brooches are most frequent. The
bracelets are either of iron or bronze and their shape is simple;
neck-rings are made of twisted bronze rods, while the necklaces consist of bronze beads or of glass beads with dots.

Plate 60

The period following the various Hallstatt groups bears the
name of Early La Tène and shows a further stage in the
levelling process, by advances in the sphere of decorative art,

EARLY LA
TÈNE STYLE

133

the simplification of pottery, and the propagation of a uniform iron industry. This style developed from the Hallstatt forms probably somewhere in the zone between South-East France and South Bohemia under the strong influence of trade imports of Greek and Etruscan works of art. The bronze beaked flagon bearing a motif of a siren and crouching panthers from Hradiště near Písek in South Bohemia illustrates this. But the tray to this flagon already bears an S-shaped decoration which may be of local origin. The Early La Tène style takes the abstract geometric Hallstatt patterns, and adds to them figurative and floral elements which in the ancient local tradition become mere decorative motifs. This style appears most frequently on ornaments, particularly on the magnificent brooches displaying anthropomorphic or zoomorphic masks.

Plate 65

In Czechoslovak territory objects in Early La Tène style occur most often in South Bohemia, which is natural considering its geographical position. This style was restricted not only locally but also socially: it was the prerogative of a certain social class which can be defined as princely. The lower ranks of society at that time still lived entirely in the Hallstatt culture.

Another important innovation of that period is pottery produced on the rapidly revolving potter's wheel. This pottery comprises two fundamental forms: the bottle with a narrow neck and a globular body, and the shallow, plate-like bowl. Both are imitations of the former local hand-manufactured forms now adapted to the technology of the new method. They sometimes show a stamped decoration derived from the Early La Tène style. In the settlements they form only an insignificant part of the finds: the greater part (pots, bowls) is hand-made as in the preceding Hallstatt period.

In the region of the South and South-West Bohemian tumuli we find not only hill-forts with stone walls from this period but also barrows. Their rich equipment does not equal that of the contemporaneous South German ones but they do contain boat-shaped ear-rings in gold, brooches embellished with human or animal masks, and other articles in the Early La Tène style. There occur also flat discoid mountings decorated with human masks and swords with hilts in the shape of human figures.

Fig. 40

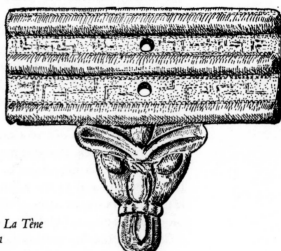

Fig. 40   Bronze girdle ornament. Early La Tène period. Želkovice, Central Bohemia. 1 : 1

In South Bohemia a contemporary culture with flat crema-tion graves is called the Hořejany type. Its graves are rela-tively poor and contain, besides pottery following Hallstatt traditions, some wheel-turned vessels, yellow beads with blue-white dots, and a La Tène brooch with a bird-mask. It is probable that these graves belong, at least partly, to the lower classes of a society whose chieftains are buried in barrows with Early La Tène equipment.

In Central and North-West Bohemia, too, we find isolated Early La Tène barrows with mask brooches and other works of art. But these are greatly outnumbered by flat cremation graves of the type called 'Cítoliby'. Here, besides pottery betraying Bylany traditions, we again meet yellow beads with blue-white dots and a brooch with a bird-mask.

Plate 69

The Turnov type in North-East Bohemia, the former territory of the Platěnice culture, displays a similar character. But in this period the assimilation of the various regions has reached such a degree that, with our present knowledge of the material, we are not certain whether the Turnov type also represents a purely local development.

Plate 64

In Moravia the Horákov culture finds further continuation in the Early La Tène period, too. The contents of this culture group is not yet sufficiently known.

SCYTHIAN
INFLUENCE

While the Early La Tène style was thus developing the Scythian animal style arose in the southern part of East Europe under similar influences from the antique world. It, too, became to a certain degree a uniting factor and, as such, penetrated into the neighbouring regions. Coming from the east in Czechoslovak territory it got as far as South-West Slovakia. In East Slovakia and in the adjoining parts of the Ukraine and Hungary it bears the name of the 'Kuštanovice group'; in West Slovakia that of the 'Hallstatt-Scythian culture'.

The Hallstatt-Scythian cemeteries are bi-ritual. For instance, at Chotín near Komárno there were two hundred and forty-six skeleton graves, one hundred and sixteen cremation graves, and eight burials of warriors with horses. The pottery is mainly of the Late Hallstatt type: cups with handles high above their rims and barrel-shaped pots with plastic ribbons under their necks, though wheel-turned vessels are also found. The weapons show distinct eastern elements: trilobate arrow-heads and iron spears. However, swords, in contrast to the Early La Tène sphere, are lacking. The quivers terminate in ornaments typical of the Scythian style. The equestrian way of life of the population buried in the Hallstatt-Scythian cemeteries is borne out by the graves of horsemen as well as by the numerous harness-mountings. Among the ornaments we find bronze dress adornments, bracelets, lock-rings ending in serpent heads, and necklaces. The silver-plated bronze mirror is a local replica of an antique pattern. Clay stamps with geometric designs, perhaps used to print on cloths, are typical. Plate 66

This concludes our brief description of the various culture groups and their history in the Hallstatt and Early La Tène periods. These groups have many common features in the spheres of economy, organization of society and religion, and may therefore conveniently be dealt with together.

The general use of iron is the characteristic feature of the Hallstatt period. Iron objects had already appeared in isolated finds in the preceding Latest Bronze Age (for example, iron spears from the Štítary type hoard at Hostomice) but were not yet universal. The first clear proofs of metallurgy exist only from the Late La Tène period, though domestic production in the Hallstatt period can hardly be doubted.

The importance of iron in advancing civilization was far greater than that of bronze, not only because its technological qualities surpassed those of bronze but also because it was more readily obtainable than either copper or tin. It is true that the smelting process is more complicated; but for the Central European metal-founders, acquainted as they were with many technological procedures in bronze-working, this difficulty was obviously not an insurmountable one. All this is evident from the rapidity of its diffusion: while it took copper and bronze at least one thousand years to come into general use, it took iron only some hundred years to supersede bronze.

In the Tumulus, Bylany, and Platěnice cultures we find axes with shaft-holes parallel to the blade, but are not sure whether they were used as weapons. Only exceptionally appears a socketed axe, such as are common in Late La Tène. Shouldered iron axes, of which we know only a few specimens, were used as tools. Iron knives were more common and the importance of the bone industry persisted.

We know more of the weapons than the tools as they were more frequently deposited in graves. All the cultures of the

Hallstatt period used iron spears and long swords of bronze or iron with scabbards ending in winged bronze shapes. Iron arrow-heads belong to this period. The fact that warfare was frequent in that period is borne out by the many hill-forts with powerful fortifications. Iron swords are also known from the Early La Tène period and objects showing the equestrian character of the warriors in the eastern regions from the Hallstatt-Scythian sphere survive.

WAGONS

The purpose of the wagons in the Hallstatt and Early La Tène periods remains obscure. Considering the lack of roads and the slight traffic we can hardly attribute any economic significance to them. Their extraordinary position in the princely graves suggests a function as war chariots, if indeed their significance was not purely symbolic.

AGRICULTURE

Agriculture complemented, especially in the less fertile regions of South Bohemia, by a more intensive pastoralism doubtless remained the principal occupation of the population. With the rare exception of sickles, iron had not yet penetrated the agricultural sphere, and we must therefore suppose that the plough and the other implements were still of wood. But, as we shall see later, growing specialization deprived agriculture of an ever-increasing number of workers, and this implies at the same time a considerable increase of productivity since it had to support many inhabitants not occupied in it. Therefore we must suppose that radical changes had taken place in agriculture but, so far, we do not know their character.

DIVISION OF LABOUR

The professional division of labour developed after the natural one through the attested appearance of the first crafts-men. They were the producers of the ornaments and other works of art of the Early La Tène. They had not only to master the complicated technique of the ornaments but also a new artistic style alien to the rustic population. It is supposed that they belonged to the trains of the chieftains for whom they worked. The maintenance of such artisans was certainly burdensome but it enabled the aristocracy to distinguish itself from the common multitude whose ornaments in the preceding Hallstatt style were produced by village founders. The existence of these first craftsmen was of no economic consequence since their activity was not a productive force, but it contained the germs of a far-reaching division of labour typical of the succeeding period.

It is difficult to solve the problem of the ownership of the fundamental means of production on the basis of archaeological discoveries. Judging by later conditions, of which we have written records, land still certainly remained common property. This can also be inferred from the fact that primary settlement had not yet come to an end and that there was still plenty of unoccupied land. We do not know whether there were any changes in the right of possession of the means of production, but we can at least be sure that plough cultivation remained the privilege of those who owned cattle.

THE DIFFER-
ENTIATION
OF SOCIETY

An important phenomenon was the universal development of the so-called princely class, of which we have innumerable proofs from the Hallstatt and Early La Tène periods. In the cemeteries of the Tumulus, Bylany, Horákov cultures and the Sered type we meet with very rich chambered tombs, sometimes covered with barrows, besides plain, flat cremation graves, some of which are also under little barrows. In some cases a difference in rite between the princely and the other graves can be observed: the former are skeleton, the latter cremation burials. In the Bylany culture the pits of the princely graves measure about four by five metres, and had been covered with a roof on which sacrificial fires were kindled. Above the wooden roof a barrow was heaped up. The uncremated body of the deceased lay in the pit on a four-wheeled wagon accompanied by numerous votive gifts: up to sixty-seven vessels, weapons, harness-mountings, and ornaments. A quarter of a pig with an iron knife, and so-called crescent symbols

(*Mondidole*) usually taken for cult-objects, also belonged to the funerary equipment.

From the Horákov culture comes another significant grave of a chieftain in the cave of Býčí skála in Central Moravia. This grave was found in 1872 and excavated unsystematically, yet it is possible to reconstruct its general picture. Under the layers covering the original surface of the cave (partly rammed down and partly paved with flat stones) were the remains of the burial, with a wagon and a great many ornaments and pottery vessels. Round about, in various positions, were forty skeletons, mostly female. Farther away, strewn over with corn, lay two human hands, decorated with bronze bracelets and gold rings, and half of a human skull. There were also bronze vessels, an ornamental sceptre, a bronze model of a bull with an iron triangle on its head, numerous bronze or gold ornaments (for example, boat and Certosa brooches), and some glass beads. There is no doubt that it was the grave of a very powerful lord with whom more than forty persons departed, hardly of their own free will, for the other world.

The equipment of these princely graves, their position in the cemeteries, and the number of persons sacrificed in the Býčí skála cave prove that the status of the persons buried in this way surpasses by far that of mere heads of patriarchal families. Weapons are one of the features of princely graves. Together with the hill-forts, and perhaps also the chariots, they bear witness to the war-like character of that time, and are probably a sign of social differentiation within the class of patriarchal overlords. It is obvious that some of these accumulated exceptional riches and power over their neighbours thus creating a separate class of 'princes'. Serfs attached to patriarchal families, who enabled the princes to cultivate a greater share of the common ground and thus maintain their martial escorts, would have formed their economic basis. The existence of such escorts, living on the labour of the rest, is made probable both by the military background and by analogies with other cultures where written records survive. It is a time rather resembling Homeric Greece and may be called rule by a warrior caste. It was democratic for the members of the martial retinues. For the rest it was a period of advanced social differentiation.

We have been able to follow this differentiation of society right from the Eneolithic Age when the first distinctions between the head and the other members of the patriarchal family began. Now in the period of the warrior caste further distinctions developed within the leading class. It seems that blood relationship remained the basis of the organizational system. The existence of any form of State cannot be presumed; written records even from more advanced epochs show only tribal units.

The fundamental character of the religion in Hallstatt and **RELIGION** Early La Tène times is not sufficiently known even though many traces of it have survived, especially in graves. From the contrast between the luxuriously and the poorly equipped burials we can infer that, as with other prehistoric cultures, the conception of the other world was fully developed and that posthumous life was, in the imagination of the people of that time, an exact copy of earthly life. It reproduced truly all the conditions of the temporal life of the deceased: consequently also social inequality. Hence the differences in the equipments of the graves, and the human sacrifices at the burials of the chieftains.

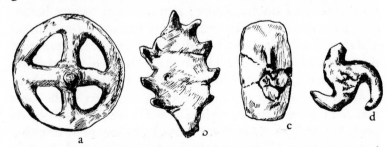

Fig. 41   Clay amulets from a tomb of the Bylany culture at Poděbrady, Central Bohemia: (a) *wheel,* (b) *oak-leaf,* (c) *shield,* (d) *triquetra.* c. 1:2

Fig. 41

Frequently we meet with various symbols whose significance we do not know: probably they are symbolic attributes of anthropomorphic deities not themselves represented in imperishable materials. Into this category belong the triquetrae painted on Bylany vessels and the little clay wheels with spokes. Both probably point to the cult of the sun, as do the water-fowl and the small suns alternating on the rim of a hammered bronze bowl belonging to the Horákov culture from the Moravian type-site. We know similar objects with the

Fig. 42

Fig. 42 Bronze pendant with water-birds drinking from a bowl. Hallstatt Tumulus culture. Hůrka-Nemějice, S. Bohemia. c. 1 : 1

motif of water-fowl and small suns from the South Bohemian Tumulus culture also. To the same culture belongs the sanctuary of Burkovák in South Bohemia. On the top of a hill on the river Vltava, in an area about twenty square metres, were found several thousand objects of fired clay: beads, coils, cog-wheels, prisms, parts of human bodies, statuettes representing horses, etc. All of them were provided with perforations for suspension and their distribution in this small area admits the interpretation that, originally, they had hung on the branches of a sacred tree. Also from the Platěnice culture come clay symbols in the shape of triquetrae, oak-leaves, etc. (probably attributes of the same deities as in the Bylany sphere), and a number of objects probably used in the course of ritual performances: drinking horns of clay, a *rhyton* in the shape of a cow, vessels on little human feet, and perhaps also clay rattles as far as they have a

Fig. 43

Fig. 43   Rattles in the shape of a pillow, a miniature vessel, and a little bird. Silesian and Platěnice cultures. Dražkovice, Skálička, and Skalice, N.E. Bohemia. 1:2

purpose in cult. Here, just as in the Bylany culture, so-called *Mondidole*, i.e. pedestalled clay crescents supposed to be of some cultic significance, often occur.

In conclusion we shall touch upon some questions of the ethnic provenance of the cultures in the Hallstatt and Early La Tène periods. We are already on the threshold of the epoch of the first written records and therefore on firmer ground than before. There is no doubt that the populations of the South Bohemian Tumulus, of the Bylany, and perhaps also of the Horákov cultures, including their successors in the Early La Tène period, were ethnically Celtic. From them we can follow a direct development to the La Tène culture which is known on the basis of written records to have been Celtic. We do not feel so certain about the Sereď type in South-West Slovakia, as it is a peripheral culture; but its origins seem to be predominately Celtic. It is not the same with the Platěnice culture, which represents the last phase of the Lausitz civilization, and had been separated from the southern culture zone of Czecho-slovakia by a distinct cultural boundary for many centuries.

THE CELTS
IN THE
HALLSTATT
PERIOD

143

This must have led to a considerable linguistic difference. There is no line of development leading from the Czecho‑slovak branch of the Lausitz culture to any known Indo‑European language group, which is why it is so difficult to determine its nationality.

THE
SCYTHIANS IN
SLOVAKIA

Ethnically the Hallstatt‑Scythian sphere in Slovakia is usually defined as Scythian. Of course, historic records tell us nothing about the residence of the Scythians in Slovakia, and it seems that many cultural phenomena of this sphere are of native origin. The only Scythian features are the armed retinues and their way of life, which could spread without any ethnic expansion. It is not impossible that this Scythian is ethnically related to the Dacian sphere, and in fact this seems indicated by the genetic relations of this culture with those of the eastern part of the Carpathian basin.

CHAPTER XII

Middle and Late La Tène: The Celts

ON THE WAY TO THE CLASS SOCIETY
FROM THE THIRD TO THE FIRST CENTURY B.C.

FROM Hallstatt times onwards it is possible to observe an ever-increasing standardization of the cultures which had reached the maximum of their ramification in the Latest Bronze Age. The La Tène culture already represents the climax of this standardization, and some of its manifestations now cover the whole southern part of Central Europe.

THE LA TÈNE CULTURE

In Czechoslovak territory the La Tène culture spread over Bohemia, Moravia, and also South-West Slovakia which had formerly belonged to the Scythian-Hallstatt sphere. In Bohemia and Moravia it developed gradually from the native Early La Tène culture, while in South-West Slovakia it probably represents an ethnic expansion from the neighbouring western regions. In the later phases material remains of the La Tène are found distributed as far as East Slovakia, where they are in some relation to the Dacian culture.

Sometimes it is assumed that the La Tène culture, as represented by the flat inhumation cemeteries, penetrated into Bohemia and Moravia from the west and represents the first arrival of the historic Celts who afterwards lived in the country alongside the older native non-Celtic population. If the question is judged exclusively from iron and bronze objects from the cemeteries, appearances support this assumption. But the earliest finds, particularly pottery, bear witness to the local development of the Early La Tène culture. The sudden appearance of the flat skeleton burials of the La Tène warriors is the result of changes in society and cult which had matured over several centuries,

ORIGINS

not of an ethnic expansion. The rich variety of metal goods could not have appeared in the material remains of the preceding period, as the strict cremation rite made it impossible. Without inhumation cemeteries from the Middle La Tène period we should know little more of its rich culture than we do of the Early La Tène period. Indeed, such is the picture of the Middle and Late La Tène in South Bohemia where large inhumation cemeteries are lacking, obviously in consequence of different prescriptions of the rite, that the culture of the Celts of this region appears poorer and in closer connexion with the Early La Tène period.

CLASSIFICA-
TION

La Tène proper can be divided into two parts characterized by the difference in their material remains. From the older, the Middle La Tène, period we know mainly inhumation, exceptionally also cremation, cemeteries with a great many weapons and ornaments but little pottery. These cemeteries begin about the end of the fourth century B.C. and continue about two hundred years: in Moravia and particularly in South-West Slovakia longer than in Bohemia. On the other hand large hill-forts, *oppida*, are typical of the Late La Tène. These oppida represent essentially the continuation of the culture of the flat inhumation cemeteries; it is remarkable that we know only very few graves from this late period.

In spite of the close connexion between these two parts of the La Tène period proper the second part appears much more developed from the social and economic point of view.

INCREASE IN
PRODUCTIVITY

The great standardization of the culture of the La Tène period caused by the prosperous development of all the branches of production is shown distinctly in the iron industry, the ornaments, and in the wheel-turned pottery.

The production and working of iron intensified considerably in comparison to the preceding period. The ore was obtained from surface layers. It was reduced in smelting furnaces, and

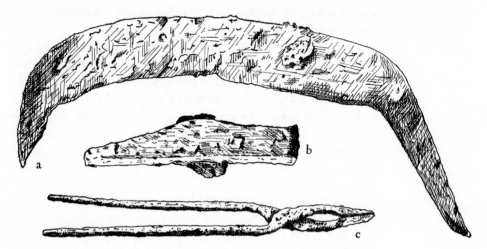

Fig. 44 Iron implements from Hradiště, near Stradonice. Central Bohemia:
(a), *scythe,* (b) *hammer,* (c) *tongs.* 1 :4, 1 : 2, 1 : 2

the red-hot iron then hammered into plates, from which
cold-beaten objects or their parts were later welded into
wholes.

Implements, especially agricultural ones, made up a great
number of these objects: ploughshares, spades, sickles, scythes.
Other kinds of implement included socketed axes, hammers,
knives, awls, chisels, saws, spoke-shaves, tongs, nails, hooks,
and chains. Except the axe, which still retained its prehistoric socketed form, all the implements already had shapes
which have persisted unchanged until recent times, which is
evidence of their functional perfection. Most of the implements
from the Late La Tène mentioned imitate patterns from the
technically maturer Roman culture, but their rapid diffusion in
barbaric Europe indicates how much they were required by the
trend of the development of that time. The mass-employment of
iron tools really exerted a revolutionary influence not only upon

Fig. 44

147

contemporary economy but through it on the basic forms of the social structure also.

WEAPONS

Fig. 45

The weapons too were made of iron; in the first place long, double-edged cut-and-thrust swords carried in scabbards with decorative mountings, and leaf-shaped spear-heads. Shields, metal-framed and with umbos in their centres, provided protection. This is the equipment of warriors as found in the flat cremation cemeteries. From the oppida come also a great number of iron arrow-heads and spurs.

Fig. 45   Iron sword, in decorated iron sheath. Jenišův Újezd, N.W. Bohemia.
c. 1:6

ORNAMENTS

Plates 67, 68

Plate 70

Ornaments appear in great numbers, in the graves of women as well as of men. Brooches form the most common ornament; sometimes there are as many as ten specimens in one woman's grave. Some are mere iron clasps but many of them, especially if made of bronze, are decorated, the bow plastically modelled and the foot set with coral or enamelled. In the Middle La Tène the foot is at first usually loose, then it is connected with the bow, while in the oppida forms the foot and the bow are cast in one piece. Torcs with seal terminals occasionally appear in graves; the torc on the neck of the deity from Mšecké Žehrovice and their appearance on coins suggest that they may have had a ritual significance. The bracelets are of bronze, often plastically modelled into hollow hemispheres or snails. Glass bracelets of simple shapes, aesthetically pleasing in their colour-scheme, are frequently found, particularly in the Late La Tène. Glass beads for necklaces were also produced. The glass was often plain, monochrome—blue, yellow, brown—or composed of these primary colours. From Central Bohemia workshops producing bracelets from shale are known.

Some of the pottery, wheel-turned vessels, was certainly manufactured by craftsmen. This production consisted mostly of bowls, flasks, pedestalled chalice-like vessels, and vases. Hand-made pottery comprised bowls with inverted rims and plain pots, barrel-shaped, with smoothed necks—both these forms are evidence of the continuance of Hallstatt traditions. In the oppida they had been wholly superseded by forms with a strong admixture of graphite and surface decorations produced with combs—technically perfect and obviously manufactured by craftsmen. This technical perfection of the La Tène pottery was obtained through the use not only of the potter's wheel but also of complicated kilns whose furnaces, divided into two parts, were separated by a grating from the actual oven in which the vessels were fired. The decoration was subordinated to the technical requirements: mostly horizontal ribs produced by turning the vessel on the wheel. In the oppida also appears pottery decorated with painted zones, sometimes plain monochrome, sometimes with latticed or other patterns. The emergence of professional production is marked by no decline from the aesthetic point of view; the shapes of the La Tène pottery are well balanced, and the profiles harmonious—accomplishments such as have seldom since been surpassed.

POTTERY

Plates 72, 73

The economic basis of the La Tène period was, as before, agriculture, now equipped, especially in the later phases, with iron implements. The new technical devices affected both the tilling of the soil and the harvest, and the prehistoric method of grinding corn into flour ended with the introduction of the rotary quern. These technical changes, probably in conjunction with the rotation of crops, give a picture of a soaring development of agriculture. The absolute and relative increase of the produce must have been substantial. It was only on the

AGRICULTURE

Fig. 46 Iron key.
Hradiště, Central
Bohemia. c. 3:4

basis of these changes in agriculture that a great social prosperity could develop.

Along with the improvement in arable farming we should
expect an advance in cattle-breeding, but of this we lack
evidence for the present. It is known that hunting was practised
and that fishing was far developed as complete sets of fishing-
tackle have been found.

So far, we know little of the settlements of the Middle La
Tène, but we can assume that they consisted of loosely connected homesteads as in the Early La Tène. Rectangular huts
with ovens within were still used. The system of the homesteads was not even abandoned in the Late La Tène, for we still
find them in the large fortified settlements called *oppida*. Oppida
belonging to the La Tène culture are known from Gaul to
Slovakia and they are everywhere typical of last century B.C.
In Bohemia there are several of them, the best known being that
near Stradonice on the river Berounka, and the largest, the as
yet unexcavated oppidum, Závist, above the river Vltava near
Prague.

OPPIDA

Plate 75

Fig. 46

The oppida occupy defensible positions, mostly above rivers,
and are strongly fortified with ditches and timber-laced stone
walls resembling those in Gaul described by Caesar as *murus
Gallicus*. The area enclosed was often arranged in terraces. On
these stood the post-built houses, covered with thatch (long
straw had become available after the recent introduction of
scythes). Near the dwellings were wells. At least some of the
houses had locks and keys.

The oppida represented a great concentration of the population, though it seems probable that sometimes their colossal
area was not wholly occupied. Handicrafts were carried on and
finds of coins prove that they were also significant as trading-
centres. Unfortunately, up to the present, they are almost the
only remains from the Late La Tène period that we have, and
it is not known what life was like beyond them.

The combination of improvements, especially in the sphere of agriculture, must have resulted in a substantial increase in the productivity of labour, which, for the first time in Central Europe, made it possible to create such a surplus that society was able to support groups of people not occupied in the production of the immediate necessities of existence.

In the Early La Tène period it is for the first time possible to speak of true craftsmen-jewellers. They were the fore-runners of the craftsmen who, particularly in the oppida, formed an important element in the community. Among them were not only jewellers using complicated glass and enamel techniques but also, and principally, smiths. The mastery of their craft is attested as much by the powerful increase in the production of iron objects as by the variety of their shapes. Finally the manufacture of pottery was also probably in the hands of specialists. Thus a new far-reaching division of labour, no longer based on principles of sex and age but on manual and intellectual abilities, set in. It is significant that those first craftsmen gathered in the oppida: it shows their close connexion with the ruling class as well as their differentiation from the rural population. Their existence was made possible by effectiveness of agriculture, but they, in their turn, were able to add to this effectiveness: thus they represent not only the consequence but also the cause of the accelerated progress of La Tène society.

CRAFTSMEN

The division of labour itself stimulated the development of a higher type of exchange. That long-distance trade, known from prehistory, persisted is proved by amber from the north and fragments of wine amphorae of southern origin found in the oppidum at Stradonice. Especially towards the end of the La Tène the trade with the south increased and brought mainly such luxury goods as metal mirrors, medical and writing implements, etc. It is most probable that the majority of these objects were acquired by means of exchange.

TRADE

THE FIRST
COINS

But a new local trade in craft-objects arose from the developed division of labour and brought the first minting of gold, silver, and bronze coins. At first, they were imitations of the tetradrachms of Philip II of Macedonia; the Celts only gradually developed their own forms of coin. Besides debased classical designs, local motifs such as boars also appear. Bohemian coins are usually ascribed to the time between the middle of the second and the middle of the first century B.C. while those from South-West Slovakia are reported from after the year 70 B.C. and are often considered as a continuation of the Bohemian coinage. This phenomenon is brought into connexion with the historically proved presence of the Boii in Pannonia. Besides iconographic motifs, inscriptions like BIATEC, NONNOS, etc. also appear on the Celtic coins from Slovakia—obviously the names of the rulers whose sovereignty they expressed. These names appear in the Latin alphabet and are the oldest epigraphic remains in Czechoslovak territory.

Fig. 47

Fig. 47   Celtic coin with the inscription BIATEC from a hoard in Bratislava.
2:1

The very important problem of the function of these coins and of the degree of their universality in trade has not yet been satisfactorily solved. The quantity of the coins found so far and their formal development do not exclude their frequent use as currency. The hoards of coins indicate that they were used for the amassing of wealth, but considering their inconstancy of weight and type it is not clear how they could have served as a measure of values. Many little balances from the oppida suggest that the coins were usually weighed in order to determine their value. The large number of different coinages reflects the instability and the lack of unity of the tribes in the La Tène period. The manufacture of coins is archaeologically attested by clay moulds not only in the oppida but also in the rural settlements.

By the end of the Hallstatt period primary colonization, except in areas particularly unsuitable for agriculture, had probably come to an end and with it also the occupation of unclaimed land. At the same time a powerful class of princes had arisen, which segregated itself more and more from the rest of the population. So far, neither the actual details of these changes nor the exact conditions of ownership during the La Tène period can be fully known. According to written records relating to the situation farther west, it seems that in the La Tène period, especially at its close, the transition to private ownership of land was already under way. SOCIAL CHANGES

In the preceding chapters it was emphasized that small tools had always been personal property. Obviously, this situation continued in the La Tène period when it acquired a new significance through the emergence of the new group of artisans. It seems that the particular status of the craftsmen, which can be inferred from finds from the oppida, developed from this right of possession. To whom the agricultural implements, particularly those of iron, belonged cannot yet be determined: most probably it was to the heads of the large families which continued to exist.

The question of the existence of slaves is still problematic; such institutions leave few archaeological traces. On the basis of SLAVES OR 'CLIENTS' written records one can assume that a small number of slaves existed at that time, but they can hardly have been of much economic importance, or they would have attracted the attention of the Roman writers. It seems more probable that the conditions described reflect the institution of 'clientship', so well known from contemporary Gaul. Former freemen, members of clans, with their families, entered the service of a more powerful person, whose protection they enjoyed in return. This institution confers on the people the right of private ownership of tools and, at the same time, creates the preconditions for the private ownership of the principal means of production—the land.

THE LEADING GROUP

At the head of society, therefore, was a group of persons which held supreme economic and political power. Obviously it developed from the 'princes' of the Hallstatt and Early La Tène periods; traces of it appear only exceptionally in the archaeological material and are distinguishable rather through the lay-out than the equipment of the graves. Ditch-encircled graves, known from South-West Slovakia, may have belonged to the members of this ruling caste. The group of warriors known from skeleton graves was numerous and formed the martial retinues to which the heads of at least some large families belonged. It is significant that in this period a great number of graves of rich women begin to appear for the first time. It supports the theory that what we have here is the transition to social classes in the sense used in the later history. The richness of the graves shows that this class must have consumed a larger share of the national income than it produced. Its privileges were probably founded on its ownership of the fundamental means of production.

THE DIS-INTEGRATION OF KINSHIP SOCIETY

The old organization of society had been established on units tied by blood relationship, but now in the La Tène period, with the changes in the sphere of interrelations of production, this principle began to break down. The concentration of those occupied with crafts in the oppida was possible only through the dissolution of the bonds tying the individual artisans to their kin—a dissolution expressed in their common residence. On the basis of a common economic activity new bonds were created.

This does not mean the sudden disappearance of the organization established on blood relationship. It is certain that some of its forms persisted among the rural population where the traditional way of living and of productive activity continued. It persisted also among the leading group as attested in historic records, but no longer bound together the two social classes which were just in formation. The former kinship organization had lost its *raison d'être*, as most of its functions connected with the protection of the individual and his rights had probably already passed into the hands of the ruling group, now taking over new functions also. Armed force was necessary for the defence of the newly-developing private property and the maintenance of overlordship. The showy martial character of the ruling group displayed in its skeleton cemeteries is therefore not surprising.

Thus crystallized slowly the preconditions necessary for the formation of a State established on a class society. Of course, it is not possible to assert that such a State already existed in the La Tène period, but decidedly it is necessary to assume that, especially in the Late La Tène, Celtic tribes in the southern part of Europe came very near to its realization. Of course, the forms of this attempt still remained based on the traditional tribal organization, even if a great part of the content was new.

In religion we must reckon with the fact that the institution of the deities, introduced by the Eneolithic patriarchal society grew stronger until a pantheon of functionally different deities had arisen. In this respect the historical reports on the western Celts give some evidence even though registered in an inadequate form by the Roman authors. Such a pantheon changed from tribe to tribe although its general character remained the

CELTIC
RELIGION

same. There are no indications that one of the deities was more important than any of the others—reflecting the fact that, so far, in real life individuals did not permanently rise above the level of the ruling group—and there were even some tribes still electing their chiefs.

Plate 74

One carving of a human head obviously representing some Celtic deity has been found in Czechoslovakia: it comes from Mšecké Žehrovice and is manufactured from local soft stone. The face is flattened, the head domed. Hair, ears, eyes, and moustache are executed in stylized elements of the ornamental La Tène style, and round the neck is a typical La Tène torc. Among religious rites, the worship of thermal springs is also attested. Evidence of it was found at Duchcov in North-West Bohemia where, when a mineral spring was deepened in 1882, a bronze cauldron was discovered. It contained more than twelve hundred objects, bronze brooches and bracelets— obviously a votive gift.

The La Tène was rich in symbolism. Bronze wheels with spokes are interpreted as symbols of the sun; perhaps they were worn as amulets. The boar, known from figurines and coins, had some religious significance. It is difficult to determine to

Fig. 48

what degree other figurines—dogs, rams, ducks, horn-blowers —were of religious significance or whether they were only manifestations of art on a small scale.

We are also at a loss for an interpretation of the traces of such operations as, for instance, trepanations. Was this perhaps based on religious beliefs? Objects interpreted as surgical instruments have been reported from the Late La Tène, and could indicate the beginning of science. Up to the present we do not have any proofs of religion other than those connected with burials, but this is only the result of the accident of survival.

The funerary conventions of the Middle La Tène period are well known from the large cemeteries. Most of the burials are inhumations but there are also cremations in bi-ritual cemeteries. In Slovakia there is even an exclusive cremation cemetery and there is the general impression that the number of cremations increased throughout the period. In the skeleton graves the bodies were usually placed on their backs with the head either to the north (in Bohemia and Moravia) or to the south (in Slovakia), but exceptions are frequent enough. Sometimes the graves were wood-lined or contained wooden coffins. Men were buried with their weapons, women with ornaments. But many graves contain very few or no votive gifts at all, and these are usually interpreted as those of the lower class of society. It is remarkable that, up to the present, we do not know of any cemetery from the Late La Tène, even in North Bohemia and Moravia: we do not know where and how the numerous population of the oppida of the Late La Tène was buried. There must obviously have been a change in the ritual conventions. On the other hand, we do know cremation graves from this period in South Bohemia. Interesting are finds of bodies without skulls or of isolated skulls in the graves. Doubt-less they give evidence of the cult of the head (*tête coupée*) that we know from western Celtic regions. The find of two skeletons and five skulls in a domestic pit on the Mužský hill in North-East Bohemia must be interpreted in the same way. Some graves were opened and obviously plundered shortly after the burial (as at Praha-Kobylisy).

Fig. 48 Bronze figu-rine of a horn player. Hradiště, near Strado-nice, Central Bohemia. 1 : 1

The character of the art of the La Tène period is pre-dominantly decorative, even though it sometimes uses religious motifs. The purpose of the jewellery was to emphasize the splendour of the ruling group; the ornaments were a form of accumulating wealth. From the ceramic objects only pottery manufactured in the way of trade on the potter's wheel and destined, as seen in the graves, for the same social group as the ornaments, expresses any aesthetic feelings. So far, the monu-mental stone head from Mšecké Žehrovice is an exception

ART

157

which is probably linked to parallels in the western Celtic world.

TOILET
ARTICLES

Among the trifles belonging to the material culture of the La Tène, toilet articles like tweezers, little spoons, and scratchers, sometimes together on a ring, deserve to be mentioned. Shaving was done with lunate razors with two terminal rings, and also little metal mirrors regarded as Roman imports have been found. Bone and bronze combs were probably used not only for combing but also for the arrangement and adornment of complicated hair-styles.

THE
PODMOKLY
GROUP

At the time just described the La Tène culture was not the only culture group in Czechoslovak territory. In North Bohemia, at the outlet of the river Elbe and dating from the Middle La Tène onwards, we have the so-called Podmokly group of cremation graves, the people belonging to which are probably rightly considered as the offspring of the local Hall-statt culture. The fundamental features of the Podmokly group are very close to the La Tène culture of North Bohemia, but nevertheless elements appear in it that connect it with the north. Obviously, it is not a Celtic, but probably a Teutonic group which, reached by a wave of Celtic La Tène civilization, had lost its ethnic characteristics.

THE
KOBYLY
GROUP

The Kobyly group of cremation graves occupied a some-what larger area in the same part of Bohemia during Late La Tène. Judging from the brooches, this group was contem-porary with the culture of the Celtic oppida, but differs con-siderably from it though retaining its fundamental La Tène character. Here appear again close relations with the north and it can hardly be doubted that it too was a Teutonic culture.

DACIAN
INFLUENCE

After the La Tène skeleton graves, there appears in both South-West and East Slovakia a culture of eastern character termed Dacian-La Tène. It can be divided into two chrono-logical phases: the first falls into the first half, the second into the second half of the first century B.C. and, as documented by the fragment of a monumental bronze statue from the settlement at Nitriansky Hrádok, is contemporary with the Roman domination of Pannonia. This group is represented mainly by pottery vessels, many forms of which are of a peculiar character as, for instance, pots with plastic decorations. Much of the wheel-turned pottery shows La Tène features and there are even painted Late La Tène vessels. The brooches found in the cremation graves under barrows belong to the Late La Tène; 'Noric' brooches of the Early Roman period are not lacking. The settlements are often fortified.

Fig. 49

Fig. 49 Pottery of Dacian character from S.W. Slovakia. Chotín and Nitriansky Hrádok. c. 1 : 10

THE PÚCHOV CULTURE

The so-called Púchov culture, so far little known, is either connected with the Dacian La Tène culture or forms its northern local group. Its material remains are reported from the valleys up to the regions of North Slovakia where, in accordance with imported Roman finds, this culture is supposed to have lasted till the second century A.D.

THE FIRST HISTORICAL REFERENCES

In the preceding paragraphs the ethnic characteristics of some culture groups have been discussed. They are partly based on written records of Greek and Roman authors referring to Central Europe. Of course, critical examination of these reports and, as far as possible, their confirmation by means of archaeological research is necessary. In general the written records speak of the migrations of the various tribes, or register simply their appearance at a certain place or a number of places. The character of these displacements is seldom mentioned: whether it was a migration of the whole population or only of a part of it, or whether it was merely a raid of warriors which, perhaps, sometimes left deeper roots. It is necessary to keep in mind that in the formation of a confederacy of tribes the name of the leading element was frequently conferred also upon them all. Many combinations and temporary situations could have existed and each could have left a different archaeological picture. Therefore archaeology will certainly be more im-portant for the establishment of the actual movements (although without names of tribes), and for the determination of their historic significance, as soon as refined research methods and sufficient material are at its disposal.

THE BOII   The earliest of the written records is attributed to Poseidonios of Rhodes and mentions that the Celtic tribe of the Boii, at the end of the second century B.C., in the region of the Hercynian Forest repulsed the attack of the Cimbri and Teutoni. This report in itself is not altogether clear, as we do not know the precise location of the Hercynian Forest. Ideas about its position seem to have changed in antiquity. Generally it is thought that this event may have occurred in the western part of Czecho-slovak territory or thereabouts. The Boii, whose name survives in Bohemia (*Boiohaemum* in Latin), perhaps inhabited part of Bohemia and were probably the bearers of the South Bohemian La Tène culture. In the south their settlements reached as far as the Danube where they were neighbours of the Vindelici; in the west they bordered on the Helvetii. Their eastern border is less distinct. Considering the report that the Marcomanni later occupied the former territory of the Boii one might assume that their settlements extended to Lower Austria and Pannonia, where the Boii in their fights with the Dacians are historically attested.

It is possible to locate another Celtic tribe by written records, the Volcae Tectosages, of whom Caesar says that they settled in the most fertile regions of Germania round the Hercynian Forest, in the northern part of Bohemia and perhaps also in Moravia. There is also linguistic evidence for the theory that this Celtic tribe got into close connexion with the Teutons, which would support the placing of it in North Bohemia. The tribe of the Cotini which lived in Moravia and is mentioned in later reports, perhaps represented the remains of the Volcae Tectosages.

VOLCAE
TECTOSAGES

The existence of the Boii in Pannonia and in South-West Slovakia is proved by their fights with the Dacians emerging from the east of the Carpathian basin: the Dacian king Boirebistas defeated the Boii in about the year 60 B.C. These facts explain the appearance of the Dacian La Tène culture in Slovakia. This is a case in which, as it seems, written and archaeological sources agree.

In this chapter has been described the colossal cultural rise of the Celtic tribes in the La Tène period. The decline of the La Tène civilization and its causes are all the more remarkable. They were partly external: the increasing restriction of the free Celtic tribes by the expansion of the Roman Empire, and the assaults of the Teutons from the north. But there were also inner forces at work. It is arguable that violent conflicts inside La Tène society developed to such a degree that it could not survive the assault from abroad.

DECLINE OF
THE LA TÈNE
CULTURE

The main significance of the La Tène civilization resides in the fact that long before any other it reached the transition from the prehistoric to the class society. This most developed feature did not find any continuation in the later development of Central Europe, which is the reason why the significance to civilization as a whole of the Celts in this area should not be over-estimated. In spite of the survival of some minor technological and artistic traditions, the cultural character of the following

SUMMARY

period of the Roman Empire is quite different. The Teutonic and then the Slavonic tribes which, in the course of the first millennium A.D., took possession of the settlement area of Central Europe, followed other ways in their development to a higher type of society than those that the Celtic tribes had taken in the La Tène period.

CHAPTER XIII

Beyond the Northern Frontiers of the Roman Empire: The Teutons

THE ROMAN EMPIRE AND THE MIGRATION PERIODS. FIRST TO SIXTH CENTURY A.D.

AFTER the decline of the Late La Tène culture in the last decades of the first century B.C. the situation in Czechoslovak territory changed fundamentally. This change was not caused by the pressure of the powerful Roman Empire upon the southern boundary of this territory but consisted mainly in the economic and social organization of the newly immigrating tribes, most of which were of Teutonic origin.

On the whole, the new organization was on a lower level than that of the preceding Late La Tène period and continued its development in a somewhat different way. Therefore it could not grow out of the former and seems rather to show a thorough change in the population, especially of the leading class. This is also confirmed from the written records of Roman authors.

The immediate neighbourhood of the Roman Empire modified the culture of the native population in many respects but was of no decisive significance in its formation. Much more important was the inner situation of the Teutonic tribes. Ethnic dislocations from the north to the south are attested in written reports (chiefly of the campaigns of the Cimbri and the Teutoni), but for the Czechoslovak territory such documentation cannot be furnished until the end of the La Tène period.

Archaeological research shows a culture quite different from that of the Late La Tène oppida and distinctly tied to the development in Thuringia; it is found associated with Late La

DIFFERENCES FROM THE LA TÈNE PERIOD

NEW DEVELOPMENTS

Tène brooches throughout the whole of Bohemia. In the earliest phase this culture is called the Grossromstedt culture or Plañany type. It is the starting-point of a further development in the Roman period (first to fourth century A.D.) and also in the Great Migration era (fifth to sixth century A.D.) in the whole of Bohemia and in Moravia. In Slovakia the survival of the Dacian La Tène culture into the beginning of the Roman era is documented and written sources give fairly reliable evidence of the ethnic continuity of the Celtic tribe of the Cotini from the La Tène period: archaeologically, however, it has not yet been possible to offer convincing proof of this continuity.

AGRICULTURE

In the Roman and Migration periods agriculture was the principal occupation of the population. But in contrast to Late La Tène agriculture it was carried on with prehistoric tools. Iron ploughshares, scythes, and other agricultural implements, widespread in the preceding period, now disappeared. Instead of rotary, saddle querns were again used in order to grind corn into flour. In small models, finds of bones and shells, etc., we have sufficient evidence that cattle-breeding, hunting, and the raising of poultry were still carried on.

TOOLS

Fig. 51

In the sphere of tools a certain improvement was achieved by the introduction of the axe with the shaft-hole parallel to the edge, a type which has continued until today. Iron spoke-shaves, shears, perhaps used for the shearing of sheep, nails, hooks, flint, and strike-a-lights are also known. Knives were common.

POTTERY

Plate 77
Fig. 50

However pottery was less developed than it was in the La Tène culture. Its most characteristic feature is that it was made without the use of the potter's wheel. In the early phase vase-like shapes appear still, but later we find bowls, most of which develop into bi-conical shapes at the time of the Migrations. High-stemmed cups of the so-called Plañany type are characteristic of the oldest phase of the pottery. In the settlements, bowls with inverted rims and barrel-shaped pots occur

Fig. 50 Beaker of the Plaňany type dated to the beginning of the Roman period. Starý Vestec, Central Bohemia. 1 : 2

Fig. 51 Iron scissors of the Early Roman period. Dobřichov, Central Bohemia. 1 : 2

most frequently, often decorated with finger-nail impressions or groups of incisions. In the early phase the pottery is usually without any decoration but sometimes there is a meander or a similar pattern executed with a toothed wheel under the neck of the vessel. In the Late Roman and Migration periods channelled decorations prevail on the bowl-shaped forms, if they are ornamented at all. Under the influence of provincial Roman pottery, jugs decorated with smoothed lattice motifs are met with from the fourth century onwards.

In the Late Roman period, mainly in the fourth century, perfect, wheel-turned, oven-fired pottery began to be produced again in West Slovakia and Moravia. It reflects probably the influence of the developed pottery of the near-by Roman provinces and therefore in Bohemia we find much slighter traces in the form of isolated vessels.

It must be realized that pottery was now losing much of its functional value through the importation of metal, glass, or

INFLUENCE OF
ROMAN
POTTERY

terra sigillata vessels. In some periods especially the table ware of the leading social class consisted mainly of these imports.

MILITARY
EQUIPMENT

The equipment of the warriors consisted of long iron swords and long spears. Wooden shields, metal-framed and provided with handles at the back and iron umbos in front, afforded protection. Spurs were already commonly used by horsemen. Other kinds of equipment are rare as, for instance, chain-mail from Očkov in Slovakia. The warriors were well armed but in encounters with the Roman army they must certainly have felt the want of specialized weapons, and particularly of organization. It is remarkable that fortifications are lacking. At the time of the Migrations not only double-edged long swords (*spatha*), but also short swords (*sax, scramasax*), were used. In this later period some weapons (mainly swords) are richly decorated with gold and precious stones. Axes, too, served as weapons; bows and arrows appear quite often. Metal helmets, some of precious metals and richly decorated, are known.

JEWELLERY

Jewellery was another craft that flourished at this time, though some of the materials formerly used (for example, glass) diminished in importance. But refined techniques in the treat-ment of metals, like granulation, filigree work, enamelling, and

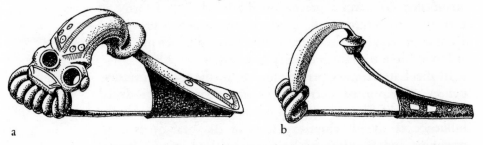

a   b

Fig. 52 Brooches of the Roman period: (a) eyelet (Dobřichov), (b) 'Noric' (Dobřichov), (c) trumpet (Nebovidy), (d) early cross-bow (Dobřichov), (e) cross-bow with high catch-plate (Dobřichov-Třebická), (f) animal (Zvoleněves). All from Central Bohemia. All c. 1 : 2 except (d) 3 : 8. (See also p. 168.)

166

in the Migration period also niello, metal inlay, chip-carving, and the setting with precious stones, made up for it. The origin of this variegated style is believed to have been in the Pontic workshops, from whence it got to Central, North, and West Europe; it is everywhere characteristic of the time of the Great Migrations.

Brooches are the most common ornament. In the early period the first decades A.D., they are derived from the Late La Tène types; the so-called Noric, and eye, brooches appear most often. Later they are joined by the so-called military brooches from the provinces, and there develop various types of crossbow brooches which are, together with the tendril brooches, the most frequent type in the Late Roman period. The tendril brooches began in East Europe, where they originated from the South Russian variant of the Late La Tène brooches. They persist until the Great Migration period. But at that time we find many other kinds of brooch—some in the shape of birds, some S-shaped, some tongs-like; finally brooches with semi-circular or rectangular heads with skittle-like projections became popular. These late brooches may be made of precious metals and decorated in chip-carving, niello technique, or set with precious stones or coloured glass. Among the less typical brooches of the Late Roman period (which are generally of foreign origin) it is necessary to mention disc and plate brooches, the latter generally being in the shape of animals.

c

d

The development of brooches is archaeologically very helpful because in their shapes they follow rapid changes of fashion, and this makes it possible to determine the age of the other accompanying material.

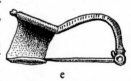

e

Among the other ornaments, we meet most often necklaces of amber, glass, or clay beads and various pendants, frequently of precious metals. In the time of the great migrations they are joined by neck- and ear-rings of valuable metals, finger-rings, and isolated bracelets. Also belt-clasps often have the character

f

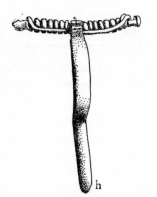

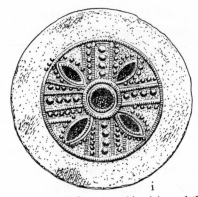

Fig. 52 Brooches from Roman period (continued from p. 167). (g) tendril (Vetlá), (h) late cross-bow (Nebovidy), (i) late discoidal (Dolínek). All from Central Bohemia. 1:3, 2:5, 5:12

of ornaments—they are decorated with open-work in the early phase, chip-carving in the Migration period. There exist bone combs decorated with engravings. Among toilet articles, often artistically decorated, tweezers and lunate razors are known.

PTOLEMY'S MAP

The map drawn up in the thirties of the second century A.D. by the geographer Ptolemy of Alexandria mentions on the territory of today's Czechoslovakia the names of numerous settlements whose identification is very difficult. We know of no large townships deserving the attention of the Alexandrine scholar and their discovery now can hardly be expected: there are not even any fortified settlements. Therefore only a few Roman stations on Czechoslovak territory (*Kelemantia, Leukaristos*, for example), can be identified with the names on Ptolemy's map.

HOUSES

The post-built houses in the settlements are generally rectangular. However, on the triumphal column of the Emperor Marcus Aurelius in Rome, celebrating the Marcomannian wars, are reliefs showing circular dwellings to which, in isolated cases, archaeologically ascertained analogies exist. Up to the present, we do not know of any settlement from the Migration period.

The general economic situation of the Teutonic tribes during the Roman and Migration periods resembles that at the time of transition from the Early to the Middle La Tène, not only in the scarcity of tools, especially those used in agriculture, but also in the state of the division of labour. It seems that the smelting and working of iron was in the hands of rustic smiths, pottery was a matter of domestic manufacture, and ornaments were the work of isolated craftsmen living with the military caste. This is evidenced by the grave of such an artisan found at Brno. The dead man was equipped with an iron spear, an axe, and a bronze helmet, and a bone comb was added. Moreover, there was a collection of tools: a little anvil, a pair of tongs, hammers, files, hooks, whetstones, unworked iron in bars and sheets, bronze balances with weights, and various bronze and iron platings. This grave shows clearly that crafts men were freemen or belonged to the ruling class at the time of the Great Migrations. ECONOMY

In contrast to the Late La Tène we observe in this period the disappearance of professional production on a large scale, especially in the field of metal-work. Thus vanishes also the significance of the smiths in the oppida in the formation of the mature La Tène civilization with an extensive market. The division of labour was inadequate, the bulk of the internal trade disappeared, and the native minting of money, now no longer necessary, stopped. It is true that we find Roman coins from that time (in Czechoslovak territory over two hundred and fifty hoards of up to a thousand coins) but these coins were not currency and probably served as a means of amassing wealth, and for the intercourse with Roman merchants who, in some periods, frequently visited barbarian territories. HOARDS OF ROMAN COINS

The differentiation in property was considerable. It manifests itself particularly in rich burials containing gold and silver PRIVATE PROPERTY objects, and collections of imported articles, especially of bronze vessels. Such rich graves are either outside the common cemeteries or form a special group within them. Moreover, these rich graves are often skeleton burials differing from the usual cremation graves. The burial at Stráže in Slovakia belonging to the fourth century can serve as an example of a rich grave. It contained twelve brooches, four silver spurs, five bronze vessels, one tripod with figural decorations, three wooden buckets with bronze and one with silver hoops, one strainer of silver, one silver bowl, two silver spoons, one bowl of *terra sigillata*, stone gaming counters, etc. Many of these objects come from provincial Roman workshops. Women as well as men were buried in these rich graves: it is evident that a real ruling class beyond the stage of patriarchal chieftains was in formation.

The transition to the private ownership of land cannot be inferred either from written or archaeological sources. According to written records it did not begin until the late phase of the Migration period, and even then it is not clear whether we can assume that the more advanced situation in the western neighbourhood of Bohemia applied also to the territories farther east: there does not seem to be enough evidence.

SLAVES   Besides conspicuously rich, 'princely' graves we also find in the cemeteries graves of average wealth belonging to the warriors of the military retinues. It is very difficult to discover archaeologically traces of the lower classes of society. The existence of a great number of slaves is not probable. It is known that the Teutons traded in slaves with Roman merchants—but not with one another. The origin of the slaves must be looked for in the many wars rather than in economic enslavement. It is probable that many of the southern products had come to the barbaric countries by way of exchange for slaves, many perhaps as Roman diplomatic bribes or as war booty. Very little of the wealth that we have described is of native origin: this is an indication of the state of under-development of the tribes in the

Roman and Migration periods as compared to the Late La Tène era.

There are no reasons for supposing that the patriarchal organization was in a state of complete decay at the time of the Roman and Migration periods. Written reports give the opposite impression. Even though there was an advanced state of disintegration it cannot be compared to the situation in the Late La Tène. The institution of the tribes was firm, and established rather on kinship principles than on territorial bonds. Matured pre-State formations as, for example, the empire of Marobuduus, were exceptions which did not last long.

Archaeological and written sources concerning religion during the Roman and Migration periods in Czechoslovak territory are both scarce. The Teutons worshipped forces of nature and deities mentioned in the descriptions of classical authors: otherwise there remains only the evidence of the cemeteries. Thus our information concerns rather the various particular conventions than the general character of the religion. In the Roman period cremation burials are customary, the graves forming large cemeteries. The bodies were burned on a pyre with the weapons which were afterwards bent or broken: this custom was perhaps in accordance with the conception of the 'death of things' which had to die with their owner. As mentioned before, many rich graves contained uncremated bodies: sometimes the leading class was segregated from the rest even in the conventions concerned with the afterlife. Already in the Late Roman period skeleton burials had spread, and in the Migration period they were common. At that time the graves were arranged in rows and at least some of them were covered with small barrows. Some graves contained a warrior with his horse: thus for instance, at Záluží near Prague a horseman, probably a chieftain, was buried in a large chambered tomb in an open space in the centre of a cemetery of about one hundred graves. At the time of the great migrations we observe a very interesting phenomenon: the systematic plunder of many rich graves by contemporaries. This must have been a very common problem all over Europe because in the West a special law against it had to be issued. The desire for orna-ments of precious metals was strong enough to overcome fear of the dead as well as the traditional religious conceptions and conventions.

ROMANS ON
THE DANUBE

Such was, in short, the culture of the tribes which, towards the beginning of the Christian era, took the place of those with the La Tène culture in Czechoslovak territory. A second factor in the historical development of the region was the Roman Em-pire, which, shortly before the Christian era, had already shifted its frontiers into the immediate neighbourhood of the Czecho-slovakia of today. From their positions on the Danube the Romans tried to penetrate farther north into the territory of the free barbarians. But the northern barbarians had similar intentions in the opposite direction, and we find evidence of their struggles in the remains which the Roman soldiers left in a broad zone on the northern bank of the Danube. To protect themselves against the barbarian tribes the Romans provided the frontier on the Danube with a number of fortified military camps (*castra*) and lesser defence works (*castella, stationes, burgi*).

Fig. 53

In the regions around Czechoslovakia there were three camps: Vindobona (Vienna), Carnuntum (opposite the confluence of the March and the Danube), Brigetio (facing the present town of Komárno). All these camps were on the southern bank of the Danube. But before long the Romans were building lesser fortifications serving as bases for raids in a northern direction and for the better defence of the water frontier on the north bank also. Opposite the camp of Brigetio, Kelemantia (today's Iža near Komárno) was established, and opposite Carnuntum a site on the top Devín. Already in the first century Kelementia had consisted of an earth rampart

ROMAN
FORTRESSES

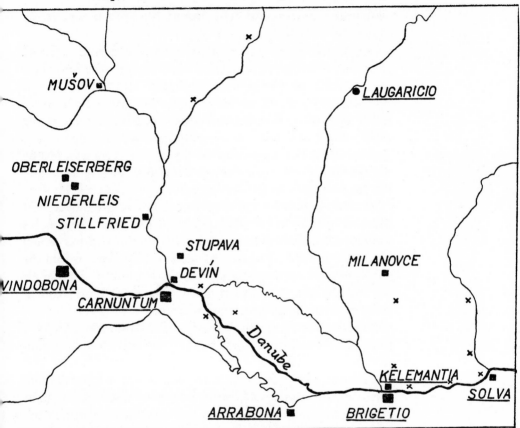

Fig. 53 Roman penetration beyond the Danube. The squares indicate castra, castella, stationes *and* burgi; *crosses indicate isolated finds of bricks on Czecho-slovak territory. The original Roman names are underlined*

with a palisade. In the second century this was replaced by a fortress built according to the usual methods of Roman military construction: a square with sides about one hundred and seventy-five metres long was encircled with a system of ditches and a wall two hundred and ten centimetres thick provided

with corner towers and eight towers between. It was reconstructed in the fourth century.

Also far in the north lesser Roman sites have been discovered.
The site at Mušov in southern Moravia and the settlement
at Stupava near Devín were of similar construction: in the
northern part a dwelling-house, in the southern a bath-house.
They were relatively small and surrounded by not very strong
walls. They were not permanently garrisoned: Stupava was
garrisoned at the beginning of the second century, Mušov
perhaps at the same time, though it is also frequently dated into
the period of the Marcomannian wars.

Recently a Roman building was found at Milanovce near
Nitra, about fifty kilometres north of the Danube. The remains
indicate a building of about twenty-one by thirty metres which
seems to have the character of a villa. It falls perhaps into the
fourth century although for its construction bricks dating from
the second century, perhaps taken from some older Roman
building in the neighbourhood, were used.

Besides these actual buildings in Czechoslovak territory a
number of stamped Roman bricks have been found, giving
evidence of further constructions in South-West Slovakia and
Fig. 54
South Moravia, for example in the ninth-century layers at Staré
Město and at Mikulčice. Considering that the distance is about
one hundred and eighty kilometres from these places to the
Danube it does not seem probable that they should have been
taken from abandoned camps in Roman provinces and used
several centuries later in the Old Slavonic constructions.
It is more probable that they come from the neighbourhood,
from some smaller Roman stations as yet unknown.

The presence of the Roman armies deep in Slovakian territory
is attested by the inscription on a rock at Trenčín: it celebrates
the victory of the Emperor Marcus Aurelius and his son
Commodus over the Teutons. The legate M. Valerius Maxi-
mianus who, somewhere in the neighbourhood, at a place

Fig. 54 Stamp of the Carnuntine manufacturer C(aius) VAL(erius) CONST(ans) KAR(nuntum) on a Roman brick from a site of the Great Moravian period at Staré Město, S.E. Moravia. c. 1 : 2

called Laugaritio (or Leugaritio; *Leukaristos* on Ptolemy's map), passed the winter of the year A.D. 179–180 with eight hundred and fifty-five soldiers of the Second Auxiliary Legion, had this inscription cut into the rock.

The activity of the Romans consisted not only in fights with neighbouring tribes and in the establishment of outposts but also in trade with tribes even far inland. This was almost exclusively in luxury goods which increased the splendour of the ruling class, very seldom in other objects. They were paid for in furs, slaves, etc.

ROMAN TRADE

Plate 76

Bronze vessels, mostly collected into drinking sets, represent the usual Roman export article. They are often luxury products of Italian workshops, the stamps of which were marked on them. So-called *paterae* with decoratively-shaped handles, buckets with ornamental handles, strainers and dippers predominate. Little jugs and bowls are rarer. A great many of these vessels date from the first century and are found in Bohemia and South-West Slovakia: afterwards the commercial relations seem to have diminished considerably, probably in consequence of the Marcomannian wars and the unsettled situation on the *limes*. More Roman goods appear again in South-West Slovakia towards the end of the third and in the fourth century.

Plate 80

Decorative pottery, pressure-moulded red vessels, so-called *terra sigillata*, were imported especially in the first half of the second century. The exporting workshops were mostly in Gaul and in the Rhineland. Their dating and the determination of provenance are facilitated as they usually bear the makers' stamp.

Plate 88

Among the glass objects, vessels from Rhenish or, less often, from Syrian workshops, were imported. Glass cups are adorned with plastic decorations or with alternating colours (so-called *millefiori* glass). They occur particularly often towards the end of the Roman period and during the Migration period.

INFLUENCE
OF THE
ROMANS

The significance of the Roman provinces did not only lie in their trade with the barbarian tribes in the north. In the territory of the provinces developed centres of production arose which partly survived the breakdown of the Roman political power on the Danube in the fourth century A.D. Thus the developed material culture of the classical world and its social slave-labour organization came into immediate proximity with the barbaric tribes. From the later symbiosis of the barbarian with the classical world originated new social patterns which could be adopted by the adjacent barbarians as soon as their economic situation enabled them to do so.

THE ETHNIC
POSITION

Shortly before the end of the first century B.C. the Romans established three new provinces on the southern bank of the Danube: Pannonia, Noricum, and Rhaetia. Already at that period they were meeting more Teutons than Celts on the Danube. It seems that the Teutonic invasion from the north into the former Celtic territory had already begun.

The fertile northern part of Bohemia was probably occupied by the tribe of the Hermunduri which lived in adjoining Thuringia also. In about the year 9 B.C. the Marcomanni, another Teutonic tribe originally inhabiting the region of the river Main, moved towards the east where it occupied the former territory of the Celtic Boii. It used to be thought that they settled at that time in Bohemia (*Boiohaemum*) where, judging by its name, it was supposed that the Boii had lived.

But in the preceding chapter it was demonstrated that the settlement area of the Boii bordered upon the Danube and that, especially in the late phases, their centre shifted more towards the east. Consequently it seems that the Marcomanni moved first in southern direction, and then down the river Danube as far as Lower Austria and South Moravia. There they occupied the territory of the Boii who had been defeated by the Dacians in Pannonia; they are mentioned no more in written sources after the arrival of the Marcomanni. This location of the Marcomanni agrees with the reports on the Marcomannian war, which was fought in the neighbourhood of the camps of Brigetio, Carnuntum, and Vindobona.

The Teutonic tribe of the Quadi, arriving perhaps contempo-raneously with the Marcomanni, probably occupied the terri-tory of East Moravia and South-West Slovakia. Shortly after the beginning of our era the Celtic tribe of the Cotini—who perhaps represent the remains of the Celtic Volcae Tectosages —are to be located in Moravia, and the Pannonian tribe of the Osi, perhaps somewhere in Slovakia.

At the beginning of the first century A.D. the Marcomanni, MAROBUDUUS under the leadership of Marobuduus, formed a strong tribal confederation against which the Romans were compelled to send twelve legions in the year A.D. 6. A rebellion in the pro-vinces interrupted the expedition but an internal conspiracy headed by Catvalda broke the power of Marobuduus. He afterwards sought protection with the Romans (who had educated him as a young man) and was of no further significance for the history of the Marcomanni. The same fate was in store for his successor Catvalda, who, not later than A.D. 21, was driven into exile by Vibilius, chieftain of the Hermunduri. Soon afterwards we learn from the written sources that the chief of the Quadi, Vannius, was superseded in the year A.D. 50 by his relatives Vangio and Sido: all of them under strong Roman influence. This Marcomannian and Quadian history

shows the precarious stability of the barbarian tribal confedera/
tions, and also how easily they succumbed to impact from
abroad. It was not possible to achieve a lasting stability as the
economic basis for it was lacking.

THE MARCO/
MANNIAN
WARS

The Marcomanni appear again in the written sources from
the year A.D. 165 on, when they attacked the Roman frontiers.
As a result the Emperor Marcus Aurelius began military
operations against them. There remains the question as to what
degree this activity was inspired by the Roman desire to extend
their power over the fertile regions north of the Danube (that is,

Plate 81

over Czechoslovak territory), where Marcus Aurelius intended
to establish the new province of Marcomannia. In the sources
these fights are called the 'Marcomannian' wars although they
mostly took place in Quadian territory, in South/West
Slovakia. The fortunes of war alternated, which was a failure for
Rome. After vain efforts the Emperor Commodus concluded
peace with the Teutons in the year 180. Then the situation on
the Marcomannian/Quadian frontiers calmed down until
the second half of the fourth century when the Emperor
Valentinian started operations deep in Teutonic territory where
he built Roman stations.

The peace on the Middle Danube after the Marcomannian
wars certainly contributed to the inner consolidation of the
Teutonic tribes but at the same time causes a silence in the
written sources. Roman interest was confined to the countries
with which she was at war or with which she traded: and even
trade diminished in this region as it increased in the western
provinces bordering upon the Teutons.

THE HUNS

There are no written reports between the Marcomannian
wars and the period of the end of the Roman power on the
Middle Danube, at the close of the fourth century. New move/
ments began with the invasion of the Turco/Tartaric Huns
from the east of the Carpathian basin, where they settled in
the territory between the Danube and the river Tisza. But they

178

also acquired Pannonia and their expeditions went far into the west. The power of the Huns was not broken by the Romans until the death of their king Attila in the middle of the fifth century. The Huns quickly adopted both Roman provincial culture and also barbarian culture. Nevertheless it is possible to recognize some of their remains. Thus, for instance, at Stráže in West Slovakia, in a grave with a Mongoloid skeleton, a Roman brooch and a little mirror showing connexions with the Caucasus region have been found. From another grave in the same locality a little provincial Roman bronze cauldron, a wheel-turned pot, and two vessels of nomadic character have been brought to light, and from a further grave a provincial Roman jug. A grave at Levice in South-West Slovakia contained a cicada-shaped brooch the origin of which must be sought somewhere far in Asia. Also other material remains, such as pedestalled bronze kettles and trilobate arrow-heads, are frequently attributed to the Huns.

At the time of the great migrations, in the present territory of Slovakia, the Teutonic Sciri also settled, perhaps only temporarily, and in the river basin of the March the Heruli, who fought the Eastern Gotones in Pannonia. Of greater significance for Czechoslovakia were the Langobardi who shifted from their settlements on the Lower Elbe to Pannonia, the frontiers of which they reached towards the end of the fifth century: before that, they had to cross Czechoslovak territory.

THE LANGOBARDI

The Langobardi are the last Teutonic tribe whose presence in Czechoslovak territory appears attested in the written sources. Judging from archaeological evidence, the Teutonic settlement lasted until the middle of the sixth century and in some areas perhaps until the beginning of the seventh. The Teutonic finds from the Migration period in Bohemia show connexions with neighbouring Thuringia, to whose sphere the Bohemian Teutons may have belonged until the destruction of the Thuringian Empire by the Franks in the year 531. But already

THE END OF TEUTONIC SETTLEMENT

from the second half of the sixth century onwards archaeological remains furnish proofs of the presence of consolidated Slavonic tribes in the whole eastern part of Central Europe, evidence which appears shortly afterwards in the written records also.

The Teutonic settlement in Czechoslovak territory lasted less than six hundred years and represents a short episode between the preceding Celtic inhabitation, which lasted more than a thousand years, and the Slavonic settlement, which occupied the country in the subsequent historical period. The culture of the Roman epoch did not continue the advanced traditions of the Late La Tène period, and therefore represents an apparent regression: but this view is not a valid one if we consider the history of the Teutonic tribes themselves; many of them matured in Czechoslovak territory so far that they were able to influence significantly the social development in the neighbouring or even in remote countries.

CHAPTER XIV

Epilogue: The Beginnings of the Slavonic Settlement of Czechoslovakia

THE ORIGIN OF THE SLAVS

IN East Germany and its neighbourhood, through the local branches of the Lausitz culture, the Teutons developed, and we have traced their characteristic culture during the Roman period in Czechoslovak territory. At the same time the oldest Slavs were emerging from the eastern area of the Lausitz culture in East Poland. Unfortunately this process has not yet been fully elucidated, as in the study of the Lausitz culture attention has been concentrated on its West Polish branches which were probably not Slavonic. Otherwise we should have to suppose a differentiation within the Slavs lasting almost three thousand five hundred years, precluded by the very small linguistic differentiation between the Slavonic nations.

Already before the beginning of the Christian era the Slavs had spread in the western part of East Europe as far as the region of the Dnieper, where their further development in the Roman period can be traced in the Zarubynci culture and some other groups. It seems that the nucleus of the Slavonic tribes that later started their expansion towards the south and the west lay just in the northern part of the Ukraine, south of the Pripet Marches and west of the Dnieper. It is difficult now to say how far the Slavs reached in the west, but in the Roman period their settlements would hardly have extended beyond the river Vistula.

The developing patriarchal society of the Roman period induced among the Slavs conditions similar to those of the   EXPANSION

Teutonic tribes. A great increase of the population must have set in which, in the system of military democracy, led to greater mobility and to the search for new settlements. At first this situation was solved by the colonization of parts of East Europe, but at the same time the first attempts at penetration were made towards the south and the west. This is indicated by certain signs in the place-names in the Carpathian basin of the Roman epoch as well as by archaeological remains. Thus, for instance, in East Slovakia certain remains from the Roman period have been found which have no connexion with the local 'Dacian' traditions but point distinctly to the development north of the Carpathian bend. With this in mind, traces of the Roman period should be searched for which can be paralleled in other regions demonstrably Slavonic at that time.

The first evidence of the presence of the Slavs south of the Carpathians is in connexion with the invasion by the Huns of the Carpathian basin. The Byzantine authors Priscus and Jordanis relate that the population offered to the Byzantine deputation on the way to Attila's court a drink called 'medos' and that a part of the obsequies at Attila's death was called 'strava'. A beverage produced from honey, *medb* enjoyed great favour with the Slavs and many Slavonic tribes still held funeral feasts called 'strava' far into the Middle Ages. Therefore one must suppose that certain Slavonic groups were already at that time in the Carpathian basin together with the Huns.

These first Slavonic penetrations into the south and west were probably of a temporary character and did not leave any distinctive traces. This can be inferred by analogy with the early expansions of the Teutonic tribes in the preceding period about which—owing to the interest of the Roman authors—we are better informed, but for which it is equally difficult to find archaeological evidence.

DIFFERENTIA- TION OF THE SLAVS

The permanent settlement of the Slavonic tribes in their historic areas did not take place until in the sixth century A.D., and it is possible to trace it archaeologically as well as partially in the written sources. It is probable that shortly before this a differentiation between the western Slavs on the one hand, and the eastern and southern on the other, had taken place in the territory between the Upper Vistula and the Middle Dnieper. The signs of it are both linguistic (closer relationship between the southern and eastern branch) and archaeological (a certain differentiation within the Old Slavonic culture at the time of expansion). Already in the sixth century the southern Slavs together with the Turco-Tartaric Avars attacked the Byzantine frontiers on the Lower Danube, across which they later penetrated even into the Peloponnese. From the region of the Lower Danube they also penetrated into the Carpathian basin and from thence they advanced northwards up to South-West Slovakia. After them we find extensive so-called Slavonic-Avaric cemeteries, in the older parts of which (as with the pottery of the 'Prague' type at Devínska Nová Ves) it is difficult to ascertain the Avaric element.

SLAVS AND
AVARS

Plates 78, 79

Plates 84, 86, 87

At approximately the same time Slavs penetrated from the north into Moravia and Bohemia, and into part of Slovakia. This colonization started from the western ancestral homeland of the Slavs and had no connexion with the attacks of the Avars.

In this way the forefathers of the Czechs and Slovaks of today came to their historic inhabitation areas. They belonged, together with the Polish, Lusatio-Serbian (Wends) and Elbe-Pommeranian tribes (Germanized in the historical period) to the western branch of the Slavs.

The earliest Slavonic culture at the time of the expansion is termed the Prague type. It spread from the West Ukraine to Bulgaria in the south, and west to Bohemia and Central Germany. Recently it has been found as far away as Olympia in Greece. The Slavonic wave which advanced towards the south already belonged to a culture in some ways distinct from

SLAVONIC
CULTURE

Plate 83

that of the western Slavs. The vessels of Prague type, though characteristic of both groups, are in the southern group associated with the coarse nomadic pottery and ornaments of the so-called Martynivka-Čadjavica group, derived from South Russian patterns at the time of the great migrations. This southern group practised both cremation and skeleton burial—for example, in the territory of South-West Slovakia.

The western group seems to have more decorated pottery while coarse nomadic wares, ornaments of the Martynivka type and skeleton graves are lacking. Settlements of this group are known from Moravia and North-West Bohemia: the huts are quadrangular, semi-subterranean and have one fireplace. Otherwise it must be admitted that present knowledge about the oldest western Slavs is incomplete. The written sources come from later periods and the archaeological remains are not very helpful. The finds consist predominantly of cremation cemeteries, in the graves of which appears usually only one urn, sometimes with a flint and steel or a knife. This explains also why the dating of the Prague type has been tentative until recently. In Rumania and Hungary metal objects date the southern variant of this culture to the second half of the sixth and to the beginning of the seventh century.

SLAVONIC
SOCIETY

The social organization of the Slavs at the time of their expansion was scarcely different from that of the Teutons in the Roman and Migration periods. Kinship ties played a decisive role, as is shown by the arrangement of the graves in the cemetery of the Prague type at Přítluky in South-East Moravia and corroborated in historical accounts. Although the scant funerary rite effaces the social differences in the cemeteries they must have continued to exist, since they had already manifested themselves in the Roman period.

The way in which the Slavonic tribes spread was connected with this type of social organization. The names of the tribes which appear often in all the three Slavonic branches (eastern, southern, western), or in two of them at least, can give us important information. Thus, for instance, the tribe of the Croats is met in all the three branches, that of the Serbs in the southern and western branches. That would indicate that the originally uniform tribe underwent in its original territory a division into several parts which, as independent units, afterwards left in search of new homes. At the same time it contradicts the theory that single families or little groups of Slavs infiltrated into the west. That the migration of the Slavs was an organized enterprise on a large scale follows from the fact that soon after it was completed, as early as the twenties of the seventh century, a powerful tribal confederation, the empire of Samo, was formed in the westernmost Slavonic territory.

The Slavonic tribes in the territory of Czechoslovakia quickly accustomed themselves to local conditions, established relations with the Byzantine and Frankish Empires and rapidly developed their own material culture. Already in the ninth century arises the Great Moravian Empire, a progressive, pre-feudal formation with a highly developed culture. At that time well fortified, powerful hill-forts, and stone churches were common in Czechoslovak territory; professional metal-working and ornament-manufacture flourished. The items of jewellery produced at that time, in the Byzantine tradition, were unequalled in contemporary Eastern Europe.

THE BEGINNINGS OF THE GREAT MORAVIAN EMPIRE

But to describe all the changes that took place after the settlement of the ancestors of the Czechs and Slovaks in their present territories would fill another volume. It is an extremely significant period, in which prehistoric society matured through social differentiation into the definite form of the first feudal state.

Fresh excavations carried out in Czechoslovakia territory after the Second World War have shed an entirely new light upon these questions; and it is archaeology that has occupied the first rank in their solution.

Bibliography

The papers marked * are published in Czech or Slovak, with summaries in English, French, or German or Italian. The titles quoted are
those of the summaries. If the work is in Czech or Slovak and has no
summary, the title is translated into English and added in brackets after
the original.

Abbreviations: *Pam Arch*=Památky archeologické.
AR=Archeologické rozhledy.
Acta MN=Acta Musei Nationalis Pragae.
Chronologie=Chronologie préhistorique de la Tchéco-
slovaquie.
Sl Arch=Slovenská archeológia.

General Publications on Prehistory

*Böhm, J., 'Study about the Periodization of the Primeval History', *Pam
Arch*, XLIV (1953), p. 1.

Childe, V. G., *The Dawn of European Civilization*, London, 1957.

Clark, J. G. D., *Prehistoric Europe: the economic basis*, London, 1952.

Engels, F., *The Origin of the Family, Private Property and the State*,
Moscow, 1954.

Morgan, L. H., *Ancient Society or Researches in the Lines of Human
Progress from Savagery through Barbarism to Civilization*, London-New
York, 1877.

Neustupný, Jiří, *Pravěk lidstva (The Prehistory of Mankind)*. Prague,
1946; Jugoslav translation, Sarajevo, 1960.

Archaeological Periodicals in Czechoslovakia

Archeologické rozhledy (Archaeological Review), from 1949, Prague.

Fontes Archaeologici Pragenses, from 1958.

Památky archeologické (Archaeological Monuments), from 1854, Prague.

Sborník Národního musea v Praze⁄Acta Musei Nationalis Pragae, from 1938.
Slovenská archeológia (Slovak Archaeology), from 1953, Bratislava.
Monumenta Archaeologica, from 1948, Prague.

Special Publications devoted to the Prehistory of Czechoslovakia

Chronologie préhistorique de la Tchécoslovaquie, Prague, 1956.
Epitymbion Roman Haken, Pragae MCMLVIII.
Kommission für das Aeneolithikum und die ältere Bronzezeit, 23–7, IX, 1958, Nitra, Bratislava, 1961.
Limes Romanus Konferenz, Nitra, 1958, Bratislava, 1959.

Previous surveys of the Prehistory of Czechoslovakia

Böhm, J, *Kronika objeveného věku (The Chronicle of the Discovered Age)*, Prague, 1941.
Eisner, J., *Slovensko v pravěku—Die Vor⁄und Frühgeschichte des Landes Slowakei—La Slovaquie à l'époque préhistorique et dans les premières périodes de l'histoire*, Bratislava, 1933.
Filip, J., *Pravěké Československo—La Tchécoslovaquie préhistorique*, Prague, 1948.
Nejedlý, Zd., *Dějiny národa českého*, I, II *(The History of the Czech People)*, Prague, 1953 and 1955.
Neustupný, Jiří—Hásek, I.—Hralová, J.—Břeň, J.—Turek, R., *Pravěk Československa (The Prehistory of Czechoslovakia)*, Prague, 1960.
Schránil, J., *Vorgeschichte Böhmens und Mährens*, Berlin⁄Leipzig, 1928.
Skutil, J.—Budinský Krička, V.—Kraskovská, L.—Eisner, J., *Slovenské dejiny (The History of Slovakia)*, Vol. I, Bratislava, 1947.

Works on the Palaeolithic and Mesolithic Periods (Chapters I–V)

Absolon, K., 'The Diluvial Anthropomorphic Statuettes and Draw⁄ings, especially the so⁄called Venus statuettes, discovered in Moravia', *Artibus Asiae*, XII (1949), p. 201.
*Bánesz, L., 'Fouilles de la station paléolithique de Seňa Cintorín', *AR*, VIII (1956), p. 625.

Czechoslovakia

*Bárta, J., 'Pleistozäne Sanddünen bei Sered' und ihre paläolithische und mesolitische Besiedlung', *Sl Arch*, V (1957), p. 5.

Klíma, B., 'Übersicht über die jüngsten paläolithischen Forschungen in Mähren', *Quartär*, 9 (1957), p. 85.

Klíma, B., 'Upper Palaeolithic Art in Moravia', *Antiquity*, XXXII, No. 125 (March 1958), p. 8.

Neustupný, Jiří, 'Le Paléolithique et son art en Bohême', *Artibus Asiae*, XI (1948), p. 214.

*Neustupný, Jiří, 'Le Paléolithique inférieur en Tchécoslovaquie', *Acta Universitatis Carolinae, Philosophica et Historica*, 3 (1959), p. 5.

*Prošek, F.—Ložek, V., 'Stratigraphische Fragen des Paläolithikums in der Tschechoslowakei', *Pam Arch*, XLV (1954), p. 35.

*Skutil, J., 'Survey of the Palaeolithic and Mesolithic Periods in Bohemia', *Acta MN*, VI–A–1 (1952).

Valoch, K., 'Beitrag zur Frage der Blattspitzen im Paläolithikum Mährens', *Germania*, 33 (1955), p. 10.

Vlček, E., 'Die Reste des Neanderthalmenschen aus dem Gebiete der Tschechoslowakei', *Hundert Jahre Neanderthaler*, p. 107, Utrecht, 1958.

Žebera, K., *Československo ve starší době Kamenné—Die Tschechoslowakei in der älteren Steinzeit*, Prague, 1958.

Works on the Neolithic Period (Chapters VI and VII)

*Neustupný, Evžen F., 'A la chronologie relative de la céramique spiralée', *AR*, VIII (1956), p. 386.

Neustupný, Jiří, 'Fortifications appartenant à la civilisation danubienne néolithique', *Archiv orientální*, XVIII, p. 131, Prague, 1950.

Novotný, B., 'Die Slowakei in der jüngeren Steinzeit', Bratislava, 1958.

*Soudský, B., 'A propos de la méthode de classer la céramique spiralée', *Pam Arch*, XLV (1954), p. 75.

*Steklá, M., 'Gliederung der Stichbandkeramik', *AR*, XI (1959), p. 211.

Stocký, A., *La Bohême préhistorique, I. L'âge de pierre*. Prague, 1929.

*Vildomec, F., 'La céramique peinte morave néolithique', *Obzor prehistorický*, VII–VIII (1928–9), p. 1, Prague.

Works on the Eneolithic Period (Chapter VIII)

*Buchvaldek, M., 'Die ältere Schnurkeramik in Böhmen', *AR*, IX (1957), p. 362.

*Hájek, L., 'Die Knöpfe der mitteleuropäischen Glockenbecherkultur', *Pam Arch*, XLVIII (1957), p. 389.

Houšťová, A., 'Long barrows of the TRB culture in Moravia', *Epitymbion Roman Haken*, p. 22.

*Kalousek, F., 'Die Glockenbecherkultur im Bezirk von Bučovice (Mähren)', *Časopis Moravského musea-Acta Musei Moraviae*, XLI (1956), p. 53.

*Mašek, N., 'Zur Frage der Řivnáč-Kultur', *Acta Universitatis Carolinae, Phil. et Historica*, 3 (1959), p. 69.

Neustupný, Evžen F., 'Die chronologischen Beziehungen des Äneolithikums', *Chronologie*, p. 66.

Neustupný, Evžen, F., 'Zur Entstehung der Kultur mit kannelierter Keramik', *Sl Arch*, VII (1959), p. 260.

Neustupný, Jiří, 'Zum Stand der relativen Chronologie des Äneolithikums in der Tschechoslowakei', *Kommission für Aeneolithikum*, Bratislava, 1961.

Neustupný, Jiří, 'Studies on the Eneolithic Plastic Arts', *Acta MN*, X–A–1/2 (1956).

*Novotná, M., 'Kupfergeräte und das Problem der ältesten Kupfergewinnung in der Slowakei', *Sl Arch*, III (1955), p. 70.

Palliardi, J., 'Die relative Chronologie der Jungeren Steinzeit in Mähren', *Wiener Prähistorische Zeitschrift*, I (1914), p. 270.

*Zápotocký, M., 'Problem der Periodisierung der Trichterbecherkultur in Böhmen und Mähren', *AR*, X (1958), p. 664.

Works on the Early Bronze Age (Chapter IX)

*Hájek, L., 'La Bohême méridionale à l'âge du bronze ancien', *Pam Arch*, XLV (1954), p. 115.

Hásek, I., 'The Early Únětician Cemetery at Dolní Počernice near Prague', *Fontes Archaeologici Pragenses*, II (1959).

Czechoslovakia

MOUCHA, V., 'Faience and glassy faience beads in the Únětice culture in Bohemia', *Epitymbion Roman Haken*, p. 44.

HNÍZDOVÁ-PLEINEROVÁ, I., 'Die Frage der Gruppen friechöfe in der Aunjetitzer Kultur', *AR*, XI (1959), p. 379.

*TIHELKA, K., 'Der Věteřov Typus in Mähren', *Kommission für Aeneo-lithikum*, Bratislava, 1961.

TIHELKA, K., 'Die Aunjetitzer Gräberfelder in Mähren', *Pam Arch*, XLIV (1953), p. 229.

*TOČÍK, A., 'Die ältere und mittlere Bronzezeit in der Südwestslowakei', *Referáty o pracovných výsledkoch čs. archeológov za rok 1955*, II (1956).

TOČÍK, A., 'Stratigraphie auf der befestigten Ansiedlung in Malé Kosihy, Bez. Štúrovo', *Kommission für Aeneolithikum*, Bratislava, 1961.

Works on the Middle, and Late Bronze Age (Chapter X)

*BENEŠ, A., 'Zu den Problemen der bronzezeitlichen Hügelgräber-kultur in Mittelböhmen', *Acta MN*, A–XIII–K–2 (1959).

*BÖHM, J., 'Die Grundlagen der Hallstattperiode in Böhmen', *Obzor prehistorický*, X (1937), p. 1.

*BOUZEK, J., 'Die Etagengefässe in Böhmen', *AR*, X (1958), pp. 345 and 548.

ČTRNÁCT, V., 'À propos des débuts de la civilisation des tumuli dans la région de Plzeň', *Chronologie*, p. 94.

*DUŠEK, M., 'Die Hallstattkultur der Chotín-Gruppe in der Slowakei', *Sl. Arch*, V (1957), p. 73.

*HRALA, J., 'Question de l'origine et extension des épées du type de Liptov et des épées à poignée en godet', *AR*, VI (1954), p. 215.

*HRALOVÁ, J., 'Zu den Problemen der späten Bronzezeit im Isergebiet', *Acta MN*, A–XI–1 (1957).

*HRUBÝ, V., 'Constructions religieuses du peuple des tumuli du Danube Moyen en Moravie', *Pam Arch*, XLIX (1958), p. 40.

*JÍLKOVÁ, E., 'Westböhmen zu Beginn der Bronzezeit', *Pam Arch*, XLVIII (1957), p. 15.

*JISL, L., 'Contribution à l'étude des débuts de la civilisation lusacienne en Tchécoslovaquie', *Českopolský sborník*, 1955, Prague.

*Kvíčala, J., 'Entstehung der schlesischen Kultur in Mähren', *Pam Arch*, XLV (1954), p. 263.

Neustupný, Jiří, 'Das Vordringen der Knobitzer Kultur nach Südböhmen', *Altböhmen und Altmähren*, 2, p. 112.

*Plesl, E., 'Zur Besiedlung Nordwestböhmens in der mittleren Bronze-zeit', *Pam Arch*, XLV (1954), p. 225.

*Podborský, Vl., 'Zu der Frage des Zusammenhanges der Entwick-lung der Urnenfelderkultur in Mähren', *Sborník filosofické fakulty brněnské university*, E–1–V (1956), p. 20.

*Říhovský, J., 'Das Problem der Expansion des Volkes mit der Lausitzer Kultur im mittleren Donaugebiet', *AR*, X (1958), p. 203.

*Spurný, V., 'Die Besiedlung von Hradisko bei Kroměříž in der mittleren Bronzezeit', *Pam Arch*, XLV (1954), p. 357.

Works on the Early Iron Age and the Early La Tène Period (Chapter XI)

*Benadík, B.—Dušek, M.—Novotný, B., contributions to the Scythia problem in Slovakia in *AR*, V (1953), p. 153; VI (1954), p. 311; VII (1955), p. 450.

Filip, J., *Popelnicová pole a počátky železné doby v Čechách—Die Urnenfelder und die Anfänge der Eisenzeit in Böhmen*, Prague, 1936–7.

*Paulík, J., 'Die südwestliche Slowakei in der jüngeren Hallstatt-periode', *Sl Arch*, IV (1956), p. 177.

*Šaldová, V., 'Flache Hallstatt-Latènezeitliche Brandgräber im böh-mischen Hügelgräbergebiet', *Pam Arch*, XLVI (1955), p. 76.

*Šolle, M., 'Südmähren in der Hallstattzeit', *Pam Arch*, XLVI (1955), p. 101.

Works on the La Tène Period (Chapter XII)

Benadík, B.—Vlček, E.—Ambros, C., 'Keltische Gräberfelder der Südwestslowakei', *Archaeologica Slovaca-Fontes*, VI (1957), Bratislava.

*Břeň, J., 'Fabrication des bracelets en sapropélite (soi disant lignite) en Bohême', *Acta MN*, A–IX–1 (1955).

*Castellin, K., contributions to Celtic coinage in Czechoslovakia in *Numismatické listy*, XII (1957), pp. 44, 96, 157; XIV (1959), pp. 3, 129, Prague.

Filip, J., *Keltové ve střední Europě—Die Kelten in Mitteleuropa*, Prague, 1956.

*Frel, J., 'La sculpture celtique de Mšecké Žehrovice', *Časopis Národního musea*, CXXII (1953), p. 30, Prague.

*Horáková-Jansová, L., 'Die latènezeitliche Graphitkeramik in Böhmen und Mähren', *Pam Arch*, XLVI (1955), p. 134.

Ondrouch, V., *Keltské mince typu Biatec—Celtic coins of the Biatec type from Bratislava*, Bratislava, 1958.

Powell, T. G. E., *The Celts* (Ancient Peoples and Places), London 1958.

Radoměrský, P.—Pochitonov, E., *Nálezy mincí v Čechách, na Moravě a ve Slezsku—Finds of coins in Bohemia, Moravia and Silesia*, I, Prague, 1955. English summary in Vol. IV, p. 25, Prague, 1958.

Šimek, E., *Poslední Keltové na Moravě—Die letzten Kelten in Mähren—Les derniers Celtes en Moravie*, Brno, 1958.

*Točík, A., 'Zur Frage der Besiedlung der Südwestslowakei zu Ende der alten Zeitrechnung', *AR*, XI (1959), p. 841.

Works on the Periods of the Roman Empire and the Great Migration (Chapter XIII)

*Břeň, J., 'Sépultures à squelettes de l'époque romaine ancienne en Bohême', *AR*, V (1953), p. 515.

Dobiáš, J., 'I Romani nel territorio della Cecoslovacchia odierna', *Gli Studi Romani nel mondo*, II, p. 61 (1935).

Kolník, T., 'Ausgrabungen auf der römischen Station in Milanovce in den Jahren, 1956–57', *Limes Romanus Konferenz*, Nitra, p. 27.

Křížek, F., 'Neue Ergebnisse der römischen Forschungen in der Tschechoslowakei', *Limes-Studien*, p. 77, Basel, 1959.

*Neustupný, Jiří, 'Contributions à l'époque de la Grande migration des peuples dans le bassin des Carpathes', *Obzor prehistorický*, IX (1930–1935), p. 11.

OLIVA, P., *Pannonie a počátky krize římského imperia—Pannonien und die Anfänge der Krisis des römischen Imperiums*, Prague, 1959.

ONDROUCH, V., *Limes Romanus na Slovensku—Il Limes Romano in Slovacchia*, Bratislava, 1938.

*RYBOVÁ, A., 'L'horizon du type de Plaňany dans les trouvailles d'habitat en Bohême', *AR*, VIII (1956), p. 206.

*SAKAŘ, V., 'Terra sigillata in böhmischen Funden', *Pam Arch*, XLVII (1956), p. 463.

ŠIMEK, E., *Velká Germania Klaudia Ptolemaia—Κλανδιου Πτολεμαιου μεγαλη Γερμανια*, I–IV. (French and German summaries.) Prague–Brno, 1930–53.

ŠNEIDROVÁ, K., 'Zur Chronologie des Plaňaner Typus', *Chronologie*, p. 153.

*SVOBODA, B., 'Bohemia and the Roman Empire', *Acta MN*, A–II (1948).

*SVOBODA, B., 'Böhmen in der Völkerwanderungszeit', *Acta MN*, A–I–1 (1939).

*ZEMAN, J., 'Römerzeitliche Holzeimer und die Frage ihrer weiteren Entwicklung', *Pam Arch*, XLVII (1956), p. 86.

Works on the Earliest Slavonic Period (Chapter XIV)

BORKOVSKÝ, *Staroslovanská keramika ve střední Europě—Die altslawische Keramik in Mitteleuropa*, Prague, 1940.

EISNER, J., *Devínska Nová Ves—Begräbnisstätte aus dem VII und VIII. Jahrhundert in Devínska Nová Ves bei Bratislava in der Slowakei*, 1952.

*NEUSTUPNÝ, JIŘÍ, 'Contribution à la chronologie de la céramique slave dans le bassin de l'Elbe', *Slavia Antiqua*, I, p. 397 (1948), Poznań.

NIEDERLE, L., *Manuel de L'Antiquité Slave*, I–II, Paris, 1923–6.

PLEINER, R., *Základy slovanského železářství a hutnictví—'Die Grundlagen der slavischen Eisenindustrie in den böhmischen Ländern'*, *Monumenta Archaeologica*, VI, Prague, 1958.

POULÍK, J., *Jižní Morava Země dávných Slovanů—South Moravia in the Old Slavonic Period*, Brno, 1950.

POULÍK, J., 'Zur Chronologie der ältesten slawischen materiellen Kultur in Böhmen und Mähren', *Chronologie*, p. 166.

Sources of Illustrations

Acknowledgement is made to the following individuals and institutions for photographs used in the plates: *Archeologické rozhledy* (*Archaeological Review*): 16, 18, 23, 29, 35, 36, 38–41, 43, 48, 59, 66, 75–80, 82, 85; Archeologický ústav Československé akademie věd, Brno (Archaeological Institute of the Czechoslovak Academy of Sciences, Brno): 53; Archeologický ústav Československé akademie věd, Praha (Archaeological Institute of the Czechoslovak Academy of Sciences, Prague), photographer J. Kleibl: 1, 2, 4, 6–15, 25, 65, 67, 68, 70, 71–4, 83; Archeologický ústav Slovenskej akadémie vied Nitra (Archaeological Institute of the Slovak Academy of Sciences, Nitra): 84, 87; *Artibus Asiae* (Ascona, 1948): 5; Národní museum, Praha (National Museum, Prague): 22, 26, 27, 30–2, 34, 37, 42, 45, 47, 50–1, 56, 60, 62, 69, 81; *Památky archeologické* (*Archaeological Monuments*): 3, 49, 55, 64; J. Poulík, *Jižní Morava Země dávných Slovanů* (*South Moravia in the Old Slavonic Period*), Brno, 1948–50: 54, 63; *The Prehistory of Czechoslovakia, Guide to the Exhibition at the National Museum, Prague*: 19, 20, 21, 24, 33, 44, 46, 47, 52, 61, 86, 88; *Slovenská archeologia* (*Slovak Archaeology*): 17, 28, 57, 58.

The Figures have been redrawn for this book by Mr Vladimír Chocholoušek, using the following sources: *Acta Musei Nationalis Pragae*: 31–3; *Archeologické rozhledy*, 7, 8, 11, 16, 49; J. Filip, *Keltové*: 40; J. Neustupný, *Náboženství pravěkého lidstva v Čechách a na Moravě*, Prague, 1940: 15, 41–3; J. Neustupný, *Pravěké umění v Čechách a na Moravě*, Prague, 1940: 9, 10, 18, 34; V. Ondrouch, *Keltské mince*: 47; *Památky archeologické* (*Archaeological Monuments*): 3, 5, 6, 17, 23, 25, 29, 30, 35, 37–8, 51; J.-L. Píč, *Le Hradischt de Stradonitz en Bohême*: 44–6, 48; H. Preidel, *Die germanischen Kulturen in Böhmen*: 50, 52; *Quartär*: 2; *Referáty—Archeologický ústav Slovenskej akadémie vied Nitra*: 20, 22; *Sborník . . . brněnske university* 54; J. Schránil, *Studie*: 24, 27; *Slovenská archeológia* (*Slovak Archaeology*): 4, 26, 28; A. Stocký, *La Bohême*: 14; B. Svoboda, *Čechy*: 52; K. Tihelka, *Průvodce po Cézaváchu u Blučiny*: 21; *Z dávných věků*: 19; K. Žebera, *Československo*: 3, 5. Figs. 12, 13, 36, and 39 were drawn from the objects themselves.

THE PLATES

1

2

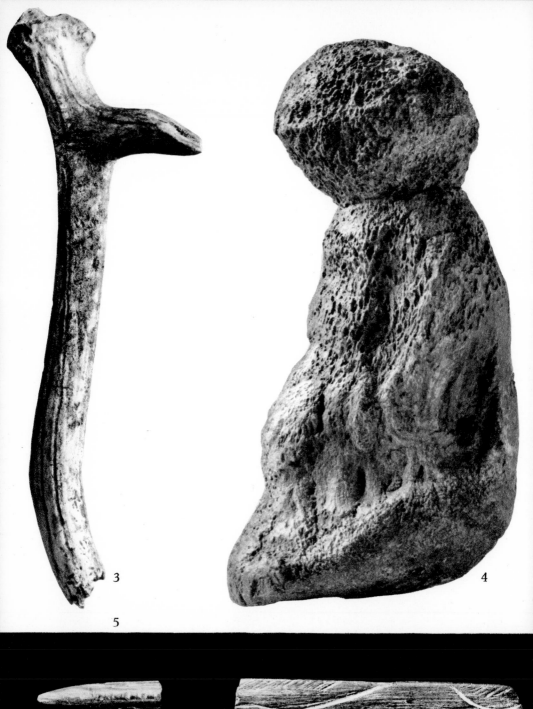

3

4

5

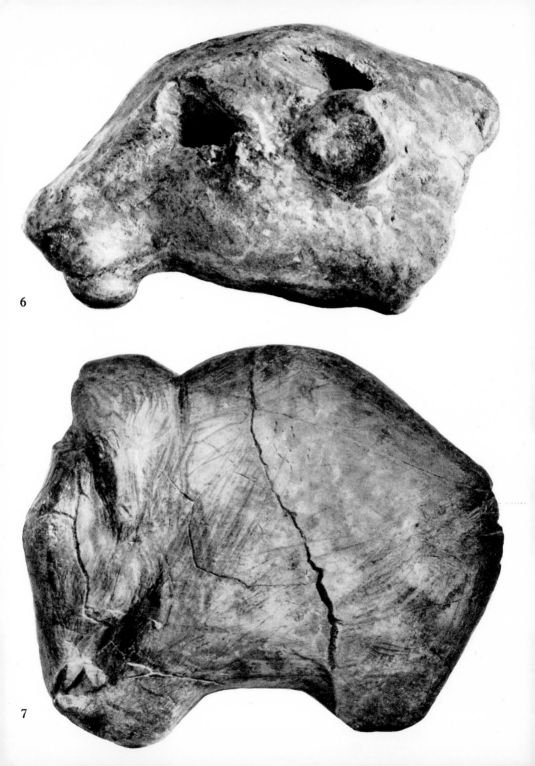

6

7

8

9

10

11

12

13

14

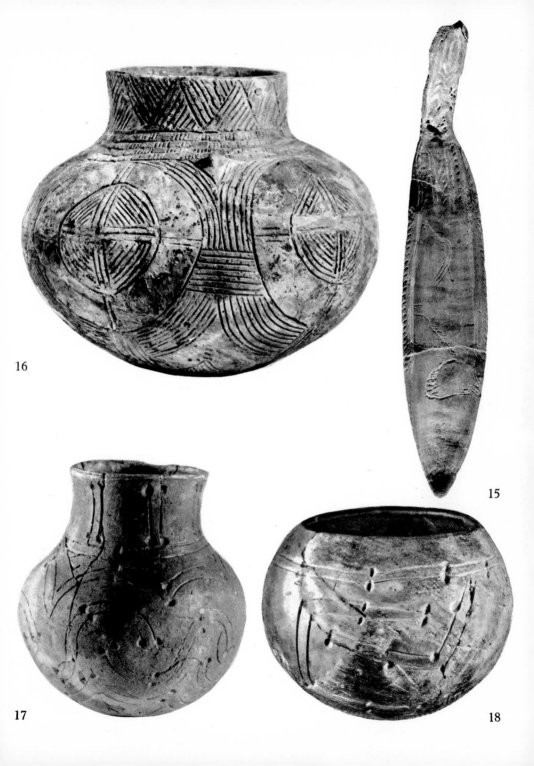

16

15

17

18

19

20

21

22

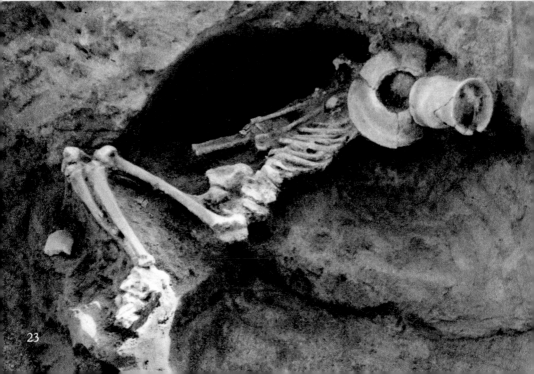

23

24

25   26

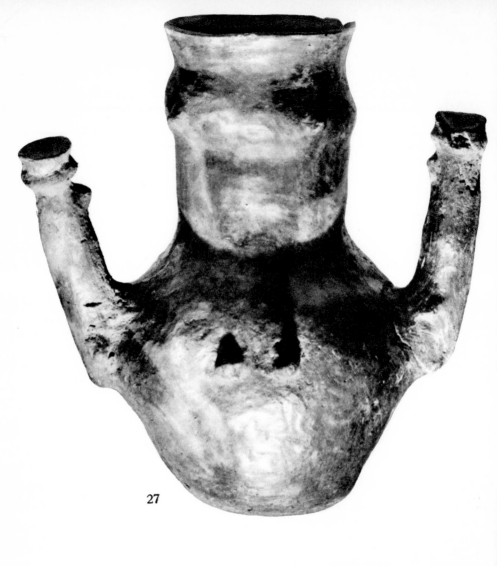

27

28

29

30

31

32

33

34

35

36

37

39

40

41

42

43

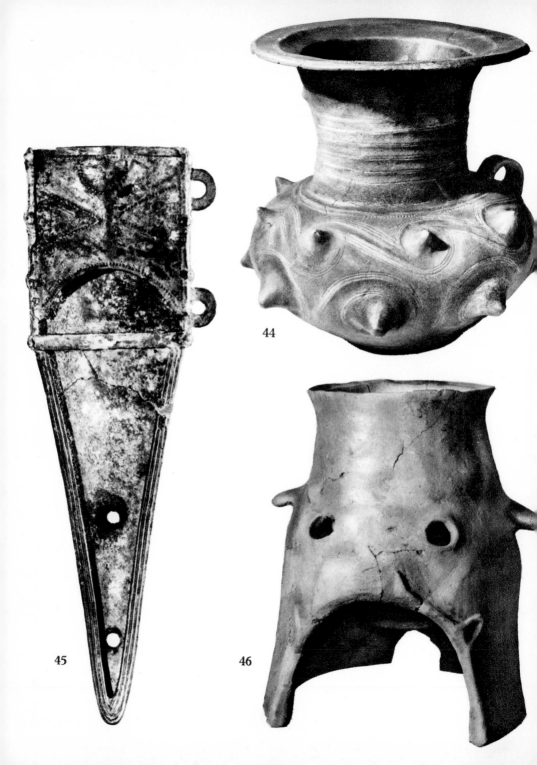

44

45

46

47

48

49

50

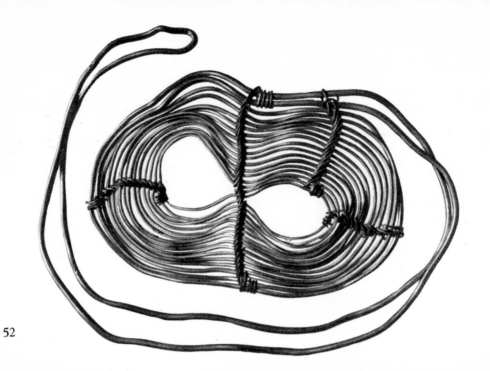

52

53

54

55

56

57

58

59

60

61

62

63

64

65

66

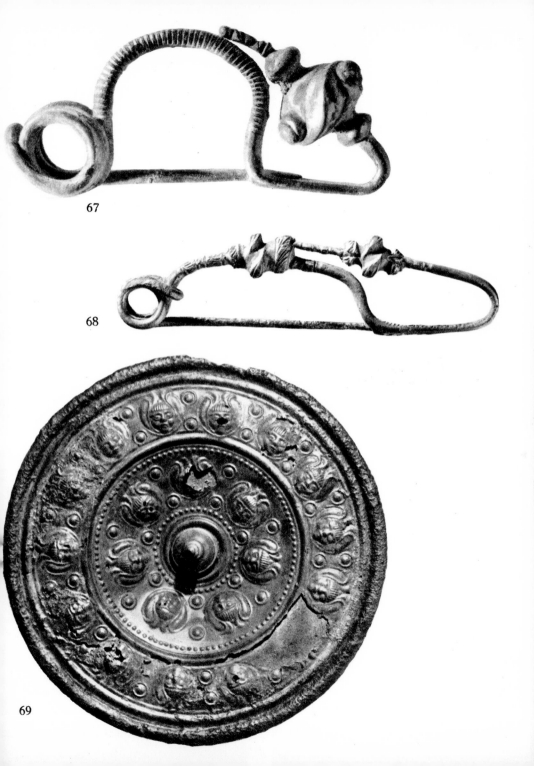

67

68

69

70

71

72

73

74

75

76

77

78

79

80

82

83

84

85

86

87

88

Notes on the Plates

1, 2 Subterranean part of two huts at Barca (E. Slovakia). Aurignacian culture. It was easier for prehistoric man to hollow part of his dwelling out of the soil than to erect it completely above ground. In Plate 1 the holes on the right are for the poles which supported the roof. As this site dates from the first Würm interstadial period of the Pleistocene, the remains of these huts discovered at Barca may be the most ancient structures known to archaeologists.

3 A pick made from reindeer's antlers and presumably used for digging, from Pavlov (S. Moravia). Gravettian culture. The Gravettians did not practise agriculture, but they needed digging tools for various purposes— to excavate the subterranean parts of their dwellings, to grub out edible roots and tubers and possibly to dig pit-traps to catch animals. This kind of pick was undoubtedly efficient, and large numbers of them have been found on the site. Length 46 cm.

4 Figurine of a woman in labour in mammoth-bone, from Předmostí (N. Moravia). Gravettian culture. All events of which the result was doubt-ful were the objects of magical ceremonies, in which figurines such as this played a part. Height 14 cm.

5 Spear-head, decorated with a stylized figure of a lamprey, from Keblice (N. Bohemia). It is made of slate and belongs to the Gravettian culture. Nothing could better show the magical purpose of the Palaeolithic hunter than the lamprey, which lives by attacking other fish. Length 14 cm.

6 Head of a bear with symbolic wound; baked clay figurine from Dolní Věstonice (S. Moravia). Gravettian culture. This is among the earliest examples of ceramic in the world. Figures like this were used in magical rites; the wound on the head was meant to enable its maker or user to succeed in the real hunt. Length 4·5 cm.

7 Mammoth figure carved in relief on mammoth tusk, from Předmostí (N. Moravia). Gravettian culture. The artistic quality of this piece is shared by other objects from sites in Moravia. Length 11·6 cm.

8 Female head in mammoth tusk, from Dolní Věstonice, unusual in having the face and coiffure (or cap?) fully portrayed. Height 7 cm.

9 Male figurine of mammoth tusk, from Brno (Central Moravia). Gravettian culture. Male figurines are unusual in Gravettian art. Scale 4:5.

10 Female figurine, the so-called Venus of Dolní Věstonice, made of ashy substance. Gravettian culture. These Gravettian 'Venuses' were clearly connected with fertility rituals—a sufficient number of children being at that time a condition of the parents' own survival. In most cases the Palaeolithic artist was interested only in those parts of the female body which best convey the idea of fertility and the head was considered unimportant. Height 11·1 cm.

11 Stylized female figurine of mammoth tusk, also from Dolní Věstonice. Gravettian culture. Length 9 cm.

12 Pendant of mammoth tusk, with engraved geometric decoration, from Předmostí. Gravettian culture. We do not know the purpose of this object—perhaps magical, perhaps merely ornamental. Length 7·5 cm.

13 Stylized female figure engraved on mammoth tusk, from Předmostí (N. Moravia). Gravettian culture. Length of figure 10·5 cm.

14 Necklace of shells and animal teeth, from Dolní Věstonice. Gravettian culture. The earliest ornaments of the human body were natural objects like those shown here, perforated and arranged to form a necklace. It was not until the Neolithic Period that ornaments were specially manufactured. In Palaeolithic cultures some magical idea is of course not excluded. Diameter *c.* 10 cm.

15 Flask-shaped vessel with incised decorations, from Šváby (N.E. Slovakia). Bükk culture. Height 13·8 cm.

16 Spatula-shaped bone object, with engraved horse figure and linear decoration, from the cave of Pekárna, near Ochoz (Central Moravia). This may have been used as a shovel, but we cannot be certain. Late Gravettian (Magdalenian). Length 28·5 cm.

17 Flask-shaped vessel with engraved spiral decoration, from Ludanice (S.W. Slovakia). Linear Bandkeramik. Height 15·5 cm.

18 Globular vessel with engraved decoration from Hurbanovo (S.W. Slovakia). Pottery becomes a standard find in all sites from the Neolithic period onwards. This vessel belongs to one of the earliest Neolithic communities in Czechoslovakia. Linear Bandkeramik. Height 9 cm.

19 Necklace of Mediterranean spondylus shells, from Kadaň (N.W. Bohemia). Linear Bandkeramik. This is more developed than the Palaeolithic necklace in Plate 14, but is still very simple. Scale 9:7.

20 Pear-shaped vessel decorated with chevrons in close rows, from Buštěhrad (Central Bohemia). Neolithic culture with Stroke Ornamented Ware. Made by the same people as the Linear Bandkeramik vessels, but the patterns are now executed by short strokes instead of the earlier incised lines. The forms of the vessels remain very simple. Scale *c.* 1:7.

21 Globular vessel with incised and encrusted decoration, from the Domica Cave, near Fiľakovo (S. Slovakia). Bükk culture. There are many examples of these beautifully decorated vessels. The incisions were originally filled in with white, giving an even greater contrast between the white pattern and the dark ground. Scale *c.* 4:5.

22 Entrance to a fortified camp of the Neolithic Lengyel culture, Hluboké Mašůvky (S.W. Moravia). View of the ditch with causeway and sleeper-trenches for wooden palisades. The pits belong to the Linear Bandkeramik culture and are earlier than the ditch and the other structures. Not all sites of this period are surrounded by ditches, and the method used raised several problems which are still unsolved; since only some of the entrances were protected by wooden structures, the fortifications could not have been very efficient. Length of ditch 35 cm.

23 Burial in contracted position, Nitriansky Hrádok (S.W. Slovakia).

Lengyel culture. The head of the dead man was covered with a pedestalled bowl, to prevent injury to the face. During the Neolithic period, cemeteries are still rare, but interment often took place in the settlements. All the Neolithic, Eneolithic, and Early Bronze Age cultures buried their dead in a contracted position. Scale *c.* 1:10.

24 Thin-walled vessel with incised and encrusted surface, from Hluboké Mašůvky (S.W. Moravia). Lengyel culture. The red and yellow colouring was applied after firing, so that it has not held on to the surface; originally this vessel must have been very beautiful. Scale *c.* 2:13.

25 Vessel showing stylized human figures made by rows of strokes, from Střelice (S.W. Moravia). Lengyel culture. On the neck are horned animals. There may be some connexion with magic. Height 38 cm.

26 Female figurine in clay, from Hluboké Mašůvky (S.W. Moravia). Lengyel culture. The precise function of these figurines, of which many specimens have been found, is unknown, but they were probably used in some sort of cult ceremony. Height 33 cm.

27 Vessel symbolizing the female body with raised arms, from Svodín (S.W. Slovakia). Lengyel culture. Although this vessel is unique, several of the clay figurines have the arms raised in a similar gesture, which may possibly indicate worship. Height 25·6 cm.

28 Copper axes from Tibava (E. Slovakia). Tiszapolgár culture. Cross-edge axes such as these are among the earliest metal implements. They are of a type known in Central Europe and in the E. Mediterranean. It is not yet known whether they were tools or weapons, or both. Scale 2:3.

29 Domed oven at Jelšovce (S.W. Slovakia). Channelled Ware culture. Similar ovens were used in other cultures. This one was probably used for cooking, as it was not high enough for the firing of pots. Length 16·5 cm.

30 Reconstruction of an Eneolithic fortified settlement at Homolka (Central Bohemia). Řivnáč culture. The settlement was a small fortified village consisting of wattle-and-daub houses.

31 Clay drum, from a grave at Brozany (N.W. Bohemia). Globular Amphora culture. A drum in this grave suggests that it belonged to a man who practised ritual ceremonies. Height 26 cm.

32 Amphora with stamped decoration at the neck, from Brozany (N.W. Bohemia). Globular Amphora culture. Scale *c.* 2:5.

33 Partitioned bowl, from Štúrovo (S.W. Slovakia). The partition down the middle of the bowl would suggest that two separate meals were served on it at the same time, but if it was used in cult rites, this explanation of course fails. Height 18·7 cm.

34 Beaker, with channelling round the neck, from Prague-Vinohrady. Corded Ware culture. In spite of the name, not all vessels of this culture have the typical corded decoration. This is a fine example of the earliest ware. Height 10·3 cm.

35 Amphora from Mouchnice (Central Moravia). Corded Ware culture. By contrast to the previous example, this is typical of the Late Moravian Corded Ware. Height 36·8 cm.

36 Slim beaker, with stamped decoration in zones, from Ledce near Brno. (Central Moravia). Bell Beaker culture. An example of the vessel from which the culture takes its name. On some specimens the decorated zones were filled with white substance which contrasted beautifully with the red background. Height 19·5 cm.

37 Beaker with stamped and encrusted decoration in horizontal zones, from Neratovice (Central Bohemia). Height 18·3 cm.

38 Burial in contracted position, at Bohdalice (Central Moravia). This is a typical burial of the Bell Beaker people. Behind the back of the skeleton there are funerary vessels and in one of them some bones of a lamb. From this we can deduce that the burial took place in early spring when lambs are born. It is one of the most accurate datings in prehistoric Europe, but we should be much happier if we knew the year or even the century of the interment instead. Scale *c.* 1:8.

39 Skull with double trepanation, from Prague-Smíchov. Únětice culture. Trepanation appears for the first time in the Eneolithic period and continues into the Early Bronze Age. We cannot be sure when it ceased, since cremation burial then became fashionable and any evidence of it would have been destroyed. The reason for its practice is still unknown, though it is clear that it was in some way connected with either the cure of mental diseases or religion or both. Perhaps the most striking fact is that some patients survived the cure, a phenomenon incomprehensible to modern surgeons. Scale *c.* 1 : 3.

40 Cup with incised and encrusted decoration, from Milovice (S. Moravia). Únětice culture. Most vessels belonging to the Únětice culture are undecorated, but highly polished. Incised decoration appears in the later phases in the eastern groups. Height 15·3 cm.

41 Contracted burial in a cist built of small stones, from Březno (N.W. Bohemia). Únětice culture. Simple pit graves are more normal in this culture, but sometimes a tomb was built of stone. The burials, however, were not substantially different. Length 140 cm.; width 90 cm.

42 Types of bronze pin, from an unknown place, Nymburk, Nehasice Neprobylice, and Lotouš (Central Bohemia). Únětice culture. Changes of fashion in the style of these pins are useful guides for dating. They were used for fastening clothes, and to prevent loss of the costly bronze objects they had at this time a little eye through which they were laced to some safer part. Scale *c.* 3 : 5.

43 Hoard of gold ornaments from Barca (E. Slovakia). Otomani culture. Barca is the only important site of this culture so far to have been excavated. Scale *c.* 1 : 1. Weight 200 gm.

44 Vessel with plastic decoration, from Barca. Otomani culture. Whereas in the western group of the Únětice culture most vessels were plain, those of the more easterly Otomani culture have both incised and relief ornament. In this vessel the patterns are produced by pressing the walls of the vessel out. Height 28 cm.

45 Bronze sheath of a dagger, from Horoměřice near Prague. Únětice

culture. At this period long swords were not known, but daggers were numerous, some of them ornamented; others were carried in decorated heaths. Length 26·4 cm.

46 Clay model of oven, from Barca. Otomani culture. These little clay ovens often appear in Bronze Age settlements, but there is considerable disagreement as to their precise function. Height 31 cm.

47 Bronze battle-axes from Křtěnov (S. Bohemia). Tumulus culture. These belong to an early stage of the culture. Though such axes were magnificent weapons they were not used very often in the Middle Bronze Age; they were replaced by long bronze swords, serving both as weapons and as symbols of power. Length of lefthand axe 23·5 cm.

48 Vessel with incised triangles, from Přítluky (S.E. Moravia). Middle Danubian Tumulus culture. Middle Bronze Age pottery is technically perfect and richly ornamented. Scale *c.* 1 : 3 cm.

49 Bronze arm-rings with decorated end-spirals, from a hoard at Staré Sedlo (S. Bohemia). Knovíz culture. The spiral was a popular form of ornament throughout the Middle and Late Bronze Age: it was sometimes engraved, but often, as here, coiled from a wire. Length 14 cm.

50 Bronze brooch with end-spirals from Jaroměř (N.E. Bohemia). Lausitz culture. Big bronze brooches of this type are typical of the Late Bronze Age, especially the Lausitz culture. Many of them seem too heavy to be worn in daily life, and may be better explained as representing social status. The central part is adorned with coiled wire which forms large even spirals on each side. Length 23·5 cm.

51 Hoard of bronze objects, as found *in situ* at Dreveník near Žehra (N. Slovakia). Piliny culture. Hoards such as this were normally deposited outside the area of prehistoric settlements and it is therefore only by good luck that archaeologists occasionally come upon them. The objects shown were hidden under a jutting rock near an abandoned site of the Eneolithic Channelled Ware. Scale *c.* 1 : 7.

52   '8-shaped' gold coil, from Černilov (N.E. Bohemia). Lausitz culture. At this time gold was probably not used as a medium of exchange. During the Bronze Age gold ornaments had the same shape, and were produced by the same technique, as their bronze counterparts. This coiled golden wire is, however, unique. It may be raw material prepared for further elaboration. Outer diameter *c.* 12 cm.

53   Casual burial under stones in a ditch of a fortified settlement, Blučina (Central Moravia). Velatice culture. Intertribal fights must have been common at this time and sometimes whole villages were massacred. At Blučina many bodies were found, some of them mutilated. It seems clear that the population was so effectively slaughtered that nobody remained to bury the dead according to the usual customs, which in this case was by cremation. Scale *c.* 1:12.

54   Vessel from Lednice (S. Moravia). Velatice culture. This is similar to Plate 55, but is mounted on human feet. It is evidence of the degree of skill achieved by the potter. Height, without handles, 8 cm.

55   Cup with high handle from Velatice (Central Moravia). Velatice culture. With its sharp profile, this cup is both technically perfect and aesthetically impressive. Height, with handle, 8·2 cm.

56   Amphora with thickened neck and channelled decoration, from Krnsko (N.E. Bohemia), showing the influence of the Knovíz culture on the Lausitz. Hundreds of such vessels have been found in the famous urn-fields, though they are not all of the same type. Height 14·7 cm.

57   Animal-shaped vessel from Chotín (S.W. Slovakia). Podolí culture. Vases shaped like animal bodies are common at the end of the Bronze Age; they presumably served some ritual purpose. Height 14·5 cm.

58   Amphora with channelled decorations, from Chotín (S.W. Slovakia). Podolí culture, in the Velatician ware tradition. Height 18 cm.

59   Bronze cups and socketed axes from a hoard at Somotor (E. Slovakia). Socketed axes are presumably of East European origin. The cups with

which they are associated at Somotor are beautifully decorated with rows
of studs. They are found in exceptionally rich graves, and may have
belonged to the dominant upper class. Length of largest axe 15 cm.

60 Horse-drawn wagon incised on a bone knife-handle, from Dobrčice
(N. Moravia). Platěnice culture. No wagon-burials have as yet been
excavated for this culture, but this engraving is proof that wagons were
used. Scale *c.* 3·1.

61 Hilt of bronze sword of the *antennae* type, from Lipovka (N.E. Bohemia).
Silesian culture. The *antennae* type of bronze sword (i.e. having two
spirals at the upper end of the hilt) is one of several types current at this
period and was widespread in Central Europe. Scale 1 : 1.

62 Vessel with geometric painting, from Straškov (N.W. Bohemia). Bylany
culture. After almost three thousand years, the practice of painting pottery
reappears in the Hallstatt period. The paint is now mostly black on well-
polished light surface; the patterns are geometric, sometimes comprising
stylized human figures. Diameter 35 cm.

63 Deep grave-pit in the middle of stone circle under a tumulus at Velatice
(Central Moravia). Horákov culture. The common people at this
period practised cremation burial, but the so-called princes were interred
in spacious log-cabins built underground and often covered by a mound.
Their bodies were uncremated and sometimes laid on wagons, the
grave being furnished with numerous pots and other objects.

64 Vessel with ribs in relief, from Střelice (S.W. Moravia). The pottery of
the Early La Tène period is coarse and poor in shape, technically perfect
for daily life but very badly produced when intended for graves. The
example illustrated is not common; simple pots and hemispherical bows
are more usual. Height 16·5 cm.

65 Relief of a winged figure on the handle of a bronze vessel from Hradiště
(S. Bohemia). Graeco-Etruscan. At the end of the Hallstatt and the
beginning of the La Tène period, Mediterranean objects began to reach
Central Europe, and helped to form the Early La Tène style. Scale 5 : 3.

66 Clay stamps, presumably for cloth-printing, from Chotín (S.W. Slovakia). Hallstatt-Scythian culture. The patterns are delicate, but we are not sure of the exact purpose of these stamps; they are peculiar to the Hallstatt-Scythian culture. Scale 4:5.

67 Bronze brooch with foot reverted to bow, from Košice (E. Slovakia). La Tène culture. The earlier ones are still embellished with human or animal motifs, but the later ones have bows segmented or notched. Length 5 cm.

68 Bronze brooch with foot reverted and fastened to bow, from Kbel (Central Bohemia). These brooches occur in all La Tène cemeteries. This belongs to the more developed Middle La Tène type. Length 13 cm.

69 Bronze disc, with human masks in relief, from Hořovičky (N.W. Bohemia). The new motifs of the Early La Tène style—such as human and animal masks—are often arranged in the old manner of the pre-historic geometrical patterns. Diameter 12 cm.

70 Bronze bracelet with round protuberances, from Rajhrad (Central Moravia). La Tène culture. These ornaments were worn either as brace-lets or round the legs and are typical of the period. Diameter 10·5 cm.

71 Bronze fitting with human mask, from Brno-Maloměřice (Central Moravia). The function of this object has been many times debated, but never settled—did it belong to a wooden vessel or to a saddle ornament? Whatever the answer, it is a beautiful example of fully formed La Tène art. Height 14·6 cm.; width 12·1 cm.

72 Pedestal vase, from Brno-Maloměřice (Central Moravia). La Tène culture. This and the next illustration show early examples of the use of the potter's wheel. At first only a small proportion of vessels were made by this process, and it was not until the later period that it became predominant. Height 23·2 cm.

73 Clay flask with plastic and incised decoration, from Veľký Grob (S.W. Slovakia). La Tène culture. Height 23·4 cm.

74 Stone head of a Celtic deity, from Mšecké Žehrovice (Central Bohemia). A rare example of monumental sculpture from the La Tène period. The eyebrows, ears, and moustaches were executed in the ornamental La Tène style, and round the neck is a typical La Tène torc. Height 25·2 cm.

75 Fortification wall made in dry-masonry technique at Hrazany (Central Bohemia), above the middle course of the river Vltava. La Tène period, a typical oppidum. In the wall are the holes for the timbers which originally supported the stones. Height of wall 75 cm.

76 Bronze figurine-ornament of a tripod, from Třebusice (Central Bohemia). Roman period. An example of Roman luxury articles imported into the Teutonic world. Height 7·8 cm.

77 Bi-conical bowl from a Teutonic burial at Smolín (S. Moravia). Great Migration period. In contrast to the developed wheel-turned pottery of the Late La Tène period, that produced during the time of the Great Migrations is mostly hand-made. Bowls like the one illustrated are typical of the third to sixth centuries A.D. Height 7·2 cm.

78 Spouted flask, of Roman tradition, from a Slavonic-Avaric cemetery at Prša (S. Slovakia). The Slavonic tribes quickly assimilated cultural elements from the territories they occupied, and, as a comparison of Plates 78 and 79 shows, copied Late Roman pottery forms. The Slavonic-Avaric culture, to which this cemetery belongs, flourished mainly in the seventh and eighth centuries A.D. At that time, however, and even later, into the Middle Ages, the typical Slavonic vessel was a simple pot decorated with incised wavy lines. Scale *c.* 2:5.

79 Slavonic vase from the same cemetery at Prša (S. Slovakia). Height 23·8 cm.

80 Objects from a grave at Prague-Bubeneč. The bronze vessels are Roman goods, the clay pot is locally made. Diameter of large bowl 36 cm.

81 Roman army crossing a river, relief from the Column of Marcus Aurelius, Rome. The scene illustrates an incident in the wars against the Marcomanni and the Quadi, and the river may possibly be the Danube.

247

The Romans never established permanent rule on the other side of the Danube, but often crossed it in campaigns against the Northern barbarians.

82 Silver brooch, originally gilded, decorated with incised patterns from Sokolnice (Central Moravia.) Great Migration period. Length 10·5 cm.

83 Urn of Prague type from Velatice (Central Moravia). Earliest culture of the Czech Slavs. Urns of this type were used in the graves of the early Slavonic tribes in Czechoslovakia. They are hand-made but of good technical quality. By the second half of the sixth century A.D. they appear in more or less the same shape throughout Central Europe and the Balkans. Height 17 cm.

84, 86, 87 Gold-plated bronze girdle-mountings from the Slavonic-Avaric cemetery at Prša (S. Slovakia). This type of ornamented girdle-mount is believed to have been introduced by the Avars. (84) Length 10·5 cm. (86) Largest mount 3·4 × 3·5 cm. (87) Diameter 2·4 cm.

85 S-shaped silver brooch from Teutonic burial, Holásky (Central Moravia). The end is a stylized bird's head, and inlaid almandines represent the eyes. In the middle of the first millennium A.D. small brooches of bronze, silver, or even gold were still the most frequent ornament; they were richly decorated by various means. Length 2·6 cm.

88 Glass vessels of Roman origin found in Teutonic graves (left to right) at Tišice and Prague. Great Migration period. True glass first appears in Czechoslovakia during the La Tène period. Glass vases were subsequently imported from the Roman Empire. Heights *c.* 16 cm., 21·3 cm., 27·5 cm.

Index

Agricultural implements: bronze, 101; iron, 147; stone, 46; wooden, 125

Agriculture: Bronze Age, 98, 125–6; Early La Tène, 138; Eneolithic, 65; La Tène, 149–50; Late Eneolithic, 82–3; Neolithic, 38, 44–6, 48; Roman period, 164

Aichbühl culture, 67

Altars, clay, Tumulus culture, 116

Amber ornaments, 82, 102, 120, 131, 167

Amphorae, 119

Animal figurines, 32, 56

Ansa cornuta, 71, 73

Arrow-heads: bone, 71, 124; bronze, 98, 116, 117, 118; stone, 27, 71, 84, 124

Art: Aurignacian, 23; Early Bronze Age, 105; Eneolithic, 74; La Tène, 157; Upper Palaeolithic, 31–2

Atlantic period, 16

Attila, 179, 182

Aurignacian culture, 22–3

Avars, 183, 247

Axe, cult of, 57

Axes: Bronze Age, 96, 117, 124, 125; iron, 137; Neolithic, 54; Palaeolithic, 18, 19; Roman period, 164

Barca, excavation at, 99, 100, 237, 242, 243

Barrows, 66, 81, 114, 119, 122

Barter, 49, 101, 103, 126

Battle-axes, 71, 76, 83

Bělá, river, 12

Bell-Beaker culture, 78–80, 90, 241

Bernburg cups, 69–70

Birch-bark cups, 95

Blučina: burials at, 117, 127, 244; hoard from, 126

Bodrogkeresztúr culture, 68

Bohemia, 11–14

Bohemian Forest, 11

Bohemio-Moravian Highlands, 11, 13, 14

Böhmerwald (*see* Bohemian Forest)

Boian culture, 53

Boii, tribe, 160, 176

Boirebistas, Dacian king, 161

Bone implements, 22, 28, 30, 54, 70, 83, 97, 125

Boreal period, 16

Bow, 27, 84

Bratislava, 15

Brigetio, Roman camp, 172, 177

Brno, 15; grave at, 169

Brno-Maloměřice, 246

Brno-Líšeň hoard, 70

Bronze Age: Early, 87–108; Middle and Late, 12, 109–28

Bronze industry, 91, 95–6, 101, 116, 117, 118, 120, 122, 124

Brooches: boat, 131; bronze, 148; Certosa, 132; double spiral, 131; drum, 132; Great Migration period, 167; harp, 131, 133; iron, 133, 148; mask, 135; Noric, 150, 167; Roman period, 167